A LITTLE BOOK OF

GOLF

ALLSORTED.

This second edition first published in Great Britain in 2025
by Allsorted Ltd, WD19 4BG, U.K.

The authorised representative in the EU is:
Petit Pop Agencies, Unit 8 Robinhood Business Park,
Robinhood Road, Dublin 22, D22 A370, Ireland
email: info@petitpop.com

The facts and statistics in this book are correct up to the end of the 2024/25 season. The data comes from publicly available sources and is presented as correct as far as our knowledge allows. The opinions in this book are personal and individual and are not affiliated to the football club in any way. Any views or opinions represented in this book are personal and belong solely to the book author and do not represent those of people, institutions or organisations that the football club or publisher may or may not be associated with in professional or personal capacity, unless explicitly stated. Any views or opinions are not intended to malign any religious, ethnic group, club, organisation, company or individual.

© Joy Gift Publishing Ltd
Author: Magnus Allan
Cover design: Milestone Creative
Contents design: Bag of Badgers Ltd
Illustrations: Ludovic Sallé

ISBN: 978-1-915902-59-7

Printed in China

Item number 5871

★ CONTENTS ★

"They call it golf because all the other four-letter words were taken."

American golfer Raymond Floyd knows the frustrations of the game.

★ INTRODUCTION ★

When you are out for a walk and you spot something roundish on the ground, there's a decent chance that you'll try to kick it. Maybe you are out with a mate, you both spot similar roundish things on the ground and you end up in a competition to see how far you can kick them. But then, maybe, you decide to add a little spice, and you both grab branches and use them to take a swipe to see how far you can hit the roundish thing.

And then, perhaps, it all gets a bit competitive and you start meeting up regularly with mates and your favourite branches to hit roundish things over the same ground, just to see how much better you might be getting. You start keeping notes on your performance, enhancing your branches so they become lighter, tougher, better. You get good at making the branches, so you start selling them to the people who have joined the game. At the same time, your mate has also worked out a way to make the roundish things actually round and fly further, and they are selling them to people as well.

Word gets out, people in other places, other lands, start doing the same thing, and before you know it, you've got an international sport that has been played on every continent of the world and is one of two sports that have been played on the Moon (the other was javelin and, no, the record doesn't count).

The origins of golf are lost in the murk of history, but that's essentially what probably happened. Og said to Zog: "I hit thing," and Zog said to Og: "I hit thing further," and it all descended into an argument until someone set up a handful of rules that let them compete against each other and themselves on a relatively level playing field, so as to speak.

Some people are happy to take a walk in a park, to while away an hour or so marvelling at nature and getting in a bit of exercise on the side. Good for them! For plenty of other people, golf offers the same benefits but makes the exercise deceptively challenging and, quite frankly, gives the walk a purpose.

Whether you are chasing the glittering lights and sponsorship deals, want to be able to add something to conversations as you hack your way around the municipal club, or simply want to get a bit of an idea about what all the fuss is about, *The Little Book of Golf* is here for you.

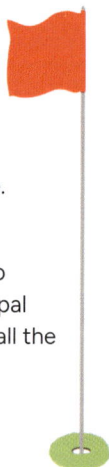

★ WHY DO YOU THINK THEY ★ CALL IT GOLF?

While the full origins of golf are indeed lost in the mists of time, and the modern game broadly emerged from the *haar* of Scotland, it's the Dutch who have the best claim to defining the game it's based on.

There are historical records dating back to around 1200 CE that talk about several games played across the Low Countries and northern France that involved a ball, a stick and a target, but these eventually coalesced into a Dutch game called 'colf' (and with that one word you can see where this is going).

Colf involved setting up a pole as a target and using a stick to try to get your ball from a starting point to the pole in the fewest number of hits. We could call them 'shots' or 'strokes' for familiarity, if you'd like.

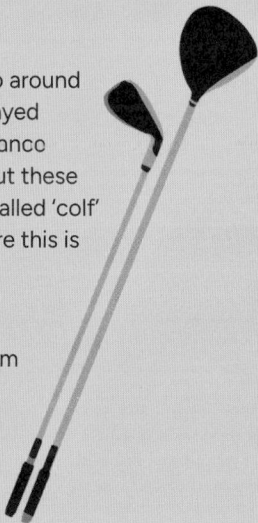

How do we know this game existed? The same way we know that any sports existed back in the day: the authorities tried to ban it. And the nice thing about authorities is that when they ban something, they tend to define it – which very much helps historians look back and say: "Oooh …"

Thou shalt not colf

Colf was banned from various places across the Low Countries because games seemed to be breaking out everywhere and anywhere. And games breaking out often meant windows getting smashed in. It was banned in Brussels at the end of the 14th century, and anyone caught playing the game would either be fined 20 shillings or have their overcoat confiscated, which was a big deal in the days before central heating. Colf was banned from the streets of Amsterdam. It was banned in both the churchyard and inside the church itself in the city of Naarden in 1456. You can tell how popular colf was with the people by how unpopular it was with the authorities.

In the winter, the game often moved out of the towns and on to the ice of frozen rivers and lakes, which is why you may see someone in a suspiciously golf-like stance in idyllic 17th century Dutch winter paintings. There are those who suggest that the sport being portrayed is ice hockey, but the fact that other people with sticks in their hands are standing watching the player addressing the ball suggests that they are waiting in turn to take a shot. If it was ice hockey, they would probably be throwing fists in at least half of the paintings.

The rules of colf in its medieval form don't survive, but from the paintings, the bans and a few bits and bobs that have survived the ravages of history, we can tell that the game was played with wooden sticks and balls made from either wood or wool wrapped in leather.

Over time, the Dutch game of colf developed into the indoor game of kolf, which was very popular in the 18th and 19th centuries. Kolf was played with longer, sturdier sticks and the balls also became larger and heavier than those used in the game of colf. At one point there were more than 350 kolf courses in the Netherlands, often tacked onto the side of a café or tavern. The game's popularity declined, though, and while there are a handful of courses left, they are mostly a local curiosity. Give it a go if you ever find yourself in the Low Countries; they'd love to see you.

Follow the trade routes

But how would a game in the Netherlands make the jump to Scotland in the 15th century? It's relatively simple: 400 years ago, roads were pretty dodgy through England, but you could hop on a boat, skip across the Channel, then hug the coast and you'd miss the worst the North Sea had to throw at you.

And because relationships between Scotland and England were frequently tepid (and often worse), there were strong trading links between Scotland and the Netherlands. As a result, the Dutch taste for colf found its way up to St Andrews, where the name evolved, the rules were localised and embellished, and it started its gentle stroll towards world domination.

I'm just off chuiwan

There is a school of thought that suggests the game of golf evolved from the Dutch game of colf, which in turn evolved from a Chinese game called chuiwan, which apparently directly translates to 'to hit a ball'. Early versions of this game were played by emperors and commoners from the Tang dynasty onwards, which started early in the seventh century CE.

By all accounts, chuiwan involved hitting a ball with a stick into a hole, which is certainly a similarity to modern golf, but chuiwan is basically a putting game, lacking the majestic sweep of the fairways. Some of the shots were also played kneeling down or squatting, which, well, if you've ever been to Scotland in the winter, you can understand why that aspect of the game might not have caught on.

Some point to the lack of evidence of a direct link between the Netherlands and China during the period, but, at the same time, we are learning more and more about how widely goods and services spread along the silk roads during the so-called Dark Ages (stuff keeps turning up in Viking-era graves in Scandinavia that really shouldn't be there), so why wouldn't games spread in the same way?

The thing is, though, there are all sorts of games around the world that are built around the concept of hitting round things with sticks – because it's a fairly basic human instinct. Chuiwan resembles the game on the green, but the smashed windows and irritated municipal authorities suggest that colf appears to have started out as something a bit like what we do on the fairway, so it seems a bit of a stretch that there's a direct relationship in that way. There is also very little evidence of similar games being played along the silk roads, which you might expect if there was a direct relationship between chuiwan and colf.

Ultimately, chuiwan might be a very distant ancestor of the putting game, but golf is undoubtedly a very separate thing.

BYRON NELSON
(USA)

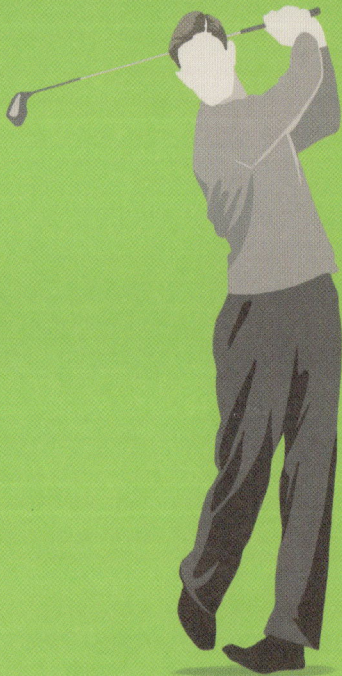

Byron Nelson crammed quite a lot into a relatively short golfing career, claiming 64 professional wins, 52 of them on the Professional Golfers' Association of America (PGA) Tour which gives him the sixth-most victories in the US. Which is not bad for someone who hung up his clubs at the age of 34 in 1946. His career straddled the evolution of the golf club's shaft from hickory wood to steel, and he was one of the first to realise that the change required an adaptation in swing.

Nelson won the Masters twice, in 1937 and 1942, the US Open in 1939 and the PGA Championship in 1940 and 1945, shortly before he reduced his golfing commitments to focus on his ranch.

It is said that he had exceptional control of the ball from the tee, but was unfailingly polite. When he arrived at a new course or for exhibitions, he would ask what the club professional's course record was, and would deliberately shoot just under out of respect.

★ THE GOLF BALL ★

Golf balls appear to have gone through four distinct phases as they have evolved into their present form: hairy-leathery, feathery-leathery, rubbery and modern(ish). Wooden balls have been talked about historically, but according to most experts, they could well be a bit of a red herring. There isn't a lot of actual evidence that wooden balls were really used once the game's development started gaining momentum in Scotland, simply a set of assumptions based on the materials around at the time and the tools and knowledge available to craft them.

It goes something like this ... When colf arrived in Scotland, it is suggested that it brought its balls with it. At the time, these were either wooden or — more likely — leather pouches filled with cow's hair or straw (the hairy-leathery).

From a performance point of view, there's a fairly big difference between a wooden ball and a leather and cow's hair ball. According to science, a wooden golf ball would only fly around 82 yards (75 metres) on a good day with the wind behind it. It also breaks easily, is inconsistent and is difficult (and for 'difficult' read 'expensive') to produce.

Leather, meanwhile, will give you upwards of 220 yards (200 metres) and is somewhat more robust. The leather had to be stitched by hand, but if you can make a leather shoe, then a leather ball is not exactly a challenge. Still expensive, but a vastly superior golfing experience.

There are records of large quantities of hairy-leathery balls being imported from the Netherlands in golf's earliest days. In fact, so many of them were being imported into Scotland in the early 17th century that James VI (who enjoyed a later career as James I of England) had to step in and get a local industry rolling because Scotland was allegedly sending so much money to the Netherlands to pay for balls that the balance of payments was being upset. And nobody's happy when the balance of payments is upset.

Hairy-leathery to feathery-leathery

The next big breakthrough came in 1618 with the introduction of the 'feathery-leathery' balls. As the name suggests, these were leather pouches – similar to the hairy-leathery balls – but they were stuffed with goose or chicken feathers. This meant that they were denser than balls stuffed with cow hair or straw, so they flew further when you walloped them with a golf club.

It wasn't just the stuffing that changed, though; there was also an innovation in the way that they were produced. Feathery-leathery balls were made while the leather and the feathers were wet. The leather contracted and the feathers expanded as they both dried, creating pressure that held the ball in shape and increasing the density so it had an even greater range when out on the course. Some have even suggested that the performance of the feathery-leathery balls has only recently been matched by the very latest modern balls.

The problem was that all this work meant that a feathery-leathery ball took more time to craft, and time means cost, so they were twice the price of their hairy precursors. This meant that for a good while both kinds of balls were flying through the air, with the hairy-leathery ones becoming known as 'common' balls.

Only happy when it rains

In truth, though, the use of leather in a golf ball had drawbacks. It needed proper looking after every time it was used if you wanted to avoid the leather splitting when it was struck by a club. There's also the fact that leather's performance suffers as it gets wet. Now, it doesn't rain every day in Scotland, but you'd be a fool not to expect some precipitation at some point in the next three minutes, so your back nine would be very different from your front nine – and looking after the golf balls must have been a major part of the regime back then.

To be fair to Scotland – and to the links form of golf, which turned the sport into a global phenomenon – while it does rain a lot on the east coast, the wind means that it also dries out very quickly, so even if you and your leathery balls get caught in a deluge, you'll likely be dried out again in a quarter of an hour. Puddles and wet grass don't hang around for too long either.

The clincher, though, is that a leather ball – hairy or feathery, wet or dry – is not that great when it comes to the delicate art of putting. In a sport like cricket, the slight inconsistencies of the ball are what makes life fascinating, but if you are faced with a long putt for a vital birdie, you want a ball that does exactly what you ask it to do. A leather ball isn't that.

The rise of the guttie

The feathery was the state-of-the-art golf ball for a couple of hundred years, until along came the esteemed Robert Adams Paterson, a native of St Andrews who was looking at his recycling one day in 1843 and decided to revolutionise golf. It was probably a Tuesday. Tuesdays are good for that sort of thing.

Paterson loved a bit of golf but wasn't a particularly well-off fellow. He couldn't afford leathery-feathery balls, so tended to play with common balls.

On the day in question, Paterson received a delivery, which was protected in a sheath of gutta-percha, a type of natural rubber derived from a tree found in Malaysia. Rather than chuck the sheath into the green bin, like a law-abiding Victorian fellow, he decided to melt it down, shape it into a sphere and take the resulting ball out for a round on the golf course.

The gutta-percha ball was a rapid success. It was cheaper, offered more consistent performance on the fairway and the green than the feathery, was harder wearing and could be remoulded if it got knocked out of shape. As any economics textbook will tell you: cheaper and better nearly always wins the day. (Economics books always contain a variety of concepts, equations, charts and models – some of them with very clever sounding names – but they all boil down to that one fact: cheaper and better nearly always wins the day. The rest of the pages are just filled with explanations of what 'nearly' means.)

In the nature of language, these new gutta-percha balls quickly became known as 'gullies', and as people used them, they found that some of the nicks and chips that happened to the ball as it was played could actually make it fly further. They were stumbling on a previously unknown thing in golf: aerodynamics.

Pretty soon, guttie-makers, which had sprung up all over the place, were adding all sorts of dents, bobbles and knobbles to the golf ball. One of the most popular types was the bramble, which had raised lumps on the surface that made it look like a blackberry (the fruit, not the executive communications device with the fiddly keyboard dating from the noughties).

Gutties were cheaper than leather balls, but there was still room for improvement. They didn't fly as well as feathery-leatheries, and at the end of a round they were often knocked out of shape, so golfers had to drop them in boiling water and then put them in a press to get them back into shape for their next round. It's not a palaver, but it is a bit of a faff.

Even so, they were much cheaper and more durable than feathery-leatheries and came to dominate golf for the next half century.

That moment in a quiet reception room

Sometimes, arrangements for a round of golf can be quite convoluted, but if you go to your golfing partner's office to wait for them before hitting the course, it's usually good manners to sit quietly in the reception room rather than draw attention to yourself. Fiddling with stuff is frowned on, and fiddling with stuff and inventing a revolutionary new golf ball and a multimillion-dollar industry seems like downright bad manners.

But that's basically what happened in Ohio in 1898. Coburn Haskell was waiting for his golfing buddy, Bertram Work, in the reception room of the B.F. Goodrich Company, a rubber-manufacturing company. It seems that rather than sit quietly, Haskell started fiddling with some rubber thread that had been left lying about, wound it into a ball and then bounced it. At which point, it nearly hit the ceiling – and Haskell had a eureka moment.

There is a version of the tale that suggests that Work invited Haskell to visit him at work because Haskell was already halfway through the process of developing what would become the Haskell ball and Work thought that the facilities at Goodrich might offer some inspiration. This version of events is less fun than the hot, burning shame of being invited to your mate's firm and then doing something to make a fool of yourself while you are supposed to be sitting quietly in the waiting room.

Either way, Haskell decided to put a cover on the rubber threaded ball, and the Haskell golf ball was born. The first few were made by hand, but another Goodrich employee, John Gammeter (who also deserves recognition for a long list of fascinating, useful and entertaining rubber inventions) developed a way to automate the winding of the thread around the inside of the golf ball, dramatically reducing the costs and increasing the speed of production.

By 1901, Haskell was able to give up the day job and focus on his side hustle. As a result, the Haskell ball rapidly replaced the guttie as the world's first-choice golf ball. One of the main reasons for this was that the Haskell is said to have offered even an average golfer an extra 20 yards (18 metres) off the tee.

The earliest versions of the ball were, by all accounts, very lively, but Walter Travis won the US Amateur Championship with a Haskell in 1901, and Alexander (Sandy) Herd won the Open Championship at Hoylake a year later, also using a Haskell. Gutties were quickly consigned to the back of the golfing cupboard.

By 1917, Haskell had become a very wealthy fellow and decided to sell off his patents, some of which were bought up by the A.G. Spalding Company.

The modern golf ball

By the 1960s, people had realised that golf ball production was a big, lucrative business and started to really turn all of the technological tools onto them. Interestingly, by this point the design was basically set, so a golf ball today looks pretty much like a golf ball from half a century ago.

Under the surface, though, there have been significant changes. The materials used have evolved and there have obviously been significant leaps in the way that they are designed and tested. The modern ball delivers a level of consistent performance that would astound our forebears.

Ironically, with the increasing recognition of the importance that balls be biodegradable, some manufacturers are turning to wood as a potential material of the future. While there is no evidence of wooden balls being used for golf in the 14th century, it may be that in the 21st century golf will start using wooden balls.

"The mechanics of my swing were such that it required no thought. It's like eating. You don't think to feed yourself,"

said Byron Nelson, reflecting on the fact that he put in so much work in the 1930s to evolve his swing for the emerging steel-shafted golf clubs that when he reached the peak of his game he didn't need to put in a lot of practice.

★ SEVE BALLESTEROS ★
(SPAIN)

If there's one name that's synonymous with European golfing in the 1980s, it's Seve Ballesteros, who announced his presence with a second-place finish in the 1976 Open Championship and was a constant on the circuit for the next two decades.

He lifted the Claret Jug as its youngest winner three years later, a victory that included a recovery shot from the car park that still gave him a birdie on the 16th. He won the Open twice more, in 1984 and 1988, as well as the Masters in 1980 and 1983. His 1980 win in the Masters was the first time the competition had been won by a European and he was, at the time, its youngest winner (although that record was subsequently broken by Tiger Woods, as almost all records inevitably are).

Ballesteros could play himself in and out of trouble seemingly at will, very often making his rounds the most entertaining of any tournament that he graced. It is said that part of the reason he was so skilled with such a variety of different strokes was because he'd only had a 3-iron to play with when he was young. If you get that good with one club, what can you achieve with a bag full?

As an Open winner, Ballesteros had the right to join the competition whenever he fancied, so in 2006 he made a brief comeback to give his son the opportunity to caddie at Hoylake.

Which is a neat way of setting the bar impossibly high for virtually every other parent in the world.

On the subject of family, Ballesteros was one of four professional golfing brothers, two of his nephews also went on to have careers in golf, and his uncle had been Spanish professional champion four times and had come sixth in the Masters in 1965. So, pedigree, basically.

Seve Ballesteros was the first player to reach the landmark European Tour official career earnings of £1 million, £2 million and £3 million. Not bad for someone who's first professional paycheque is said to have been £15.

"Everything was fine until I walked on to the first tee!"

Seve Ballesteros speaks
for each and every one
of us some days.

Player	Weeks
Seve Ballesteros (Spain)	337
Ian Woosnam (Wales)	338
Henrik Stenson (Sweden)	338
John Rahm (Spain)	342
Lee Westwood (England)	354
Justin Rose (England)	386
Nick Price (Zimbabwe)	386
Colin Montgomerie (Scotland)	400
Dustin Johnson (United States)	405
Bernhard Langer (Germany)	406
Jim Furyk (United States)	442
Adam Scott (Australia)	446
Sergio García (Spain)	453
Davis Love III (United States)	465
Nick Faldo (England)	473
Vijay Singh (Fiji)	544
Greg Norman (Australia)	646
Rory McIlroy (Northern Ireland)	763
Phil Mickelson (United States)	775
Ernie Els (South Africa)	788
Tiger Woods (United States)	906

0   100   200   300

★ WEEKS IN THE MEN'S ★ TOP 10 OF THE WORLD RANKINGS

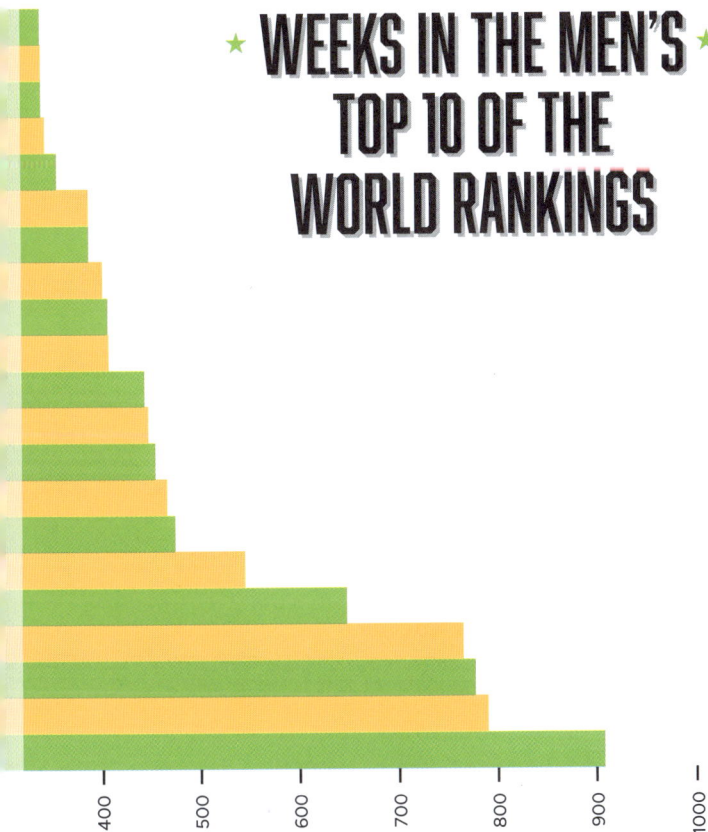

400 500 600 700 800 900 1000

⋆ WHY IS THERE SO MUCH LANGUAGE AROUND GOLF? ⋆

There are birdies and bogies, eagles and condors, there are pars and there are pins, not to mention a myriad of other random words that have come to be associated with golf. Most of them are useful, some of them are odd, but why are there so many of them?

The first reason is that slang is a useful way of passing sometimes slightly dull information between people quickly and efficiently so that you get on with the serious business of nattering about whatever else you want to talk about between holes. '1-under par' is three words, while 'birdie' is one, making it three times more efficient, assuming that everyone knows what you mean. That's not always a safe assumption, but when someone's keeping score there's always at least one other person looking over their shoulder and checking their workings, so any misunderstandings are nearly always worked out quickly and without any form of tension.

Weather also plays a role. While it would be nice to say that golfers always play in eternal late spring weather – warmed by the sun and cooled by gentle zephyrs that make the temperature just right – the reality is that sometimes it's hoofing it down and you have to shout to make yourself heard, and sometimes it's so hot out on the course that you don't want to waste precious water by speaking extraneous words. Shared slang keeps it simple.

Finally, there is also a community aspect to slang. It helps you bond with strangers and work out how deep into this golfing lark they are, which can be a useful gauge when you amble into a clubhouse looking for a game.

Every community, every industry has its own slang. If a non-golfer ever looks at you with a raised eyebrow, ask them to explain their job without using any industry-specific jargon. Bet they can't do it.

★ GIANT STEPS ARE WHAT YOU TAKE ★

US astronaut Alan Shepard was the commander of Apollo 14, the third crewed mission to land on the Moon. Apollo 13 would have been the third mission to land (after Apollo 11 and Apollo 12), but there was the whole thing with the oxygen tanks that turned into a bit of a drama, and the mission ended up being aborted.

After the tension of the previous mission, Shepard thought he'd lighten the mood a little bit and smuggled the head of a 6-iron and a couple of golf balls in with his stuff. Once they reached the lunar surface, he attached the club head to a modified (i.e. bodged) handle for a lunar rock sampler and stepped out onto the regolith to play a couple of shots. You can imagine how the folks back at Mission Control would have laughed at his high jinks.

He was somewhat constrained by his spacesuit, so ended up having to play his shots with one arm. The footage from the 1970s cameras is very grainy, but after the first shot, his crewmate commented that he'd hit more dirt than ball — because everyone's a critic, even on the Moon – but Shepard claimed to have got a clean strike on his second ball and said it went for "miles and miles and miles".

Modern analysis from the kind of people who like to take the joy out of everything suggests that his first shot went around 24 yards (22 metres) while his second did a little better with 40 yards (37 metres). Average distance with a 6-iron for a half-decent golfer is just over 155 yards (140 metres), so it seems that the disadvantage of the spacesuit outweighs the advantage of limited gravity.

Shepard's shots were the first time that golf was played on a celestial body other than Earth, but it was not the first time someone exaggerated their performance. It really was an out of this world shot though.

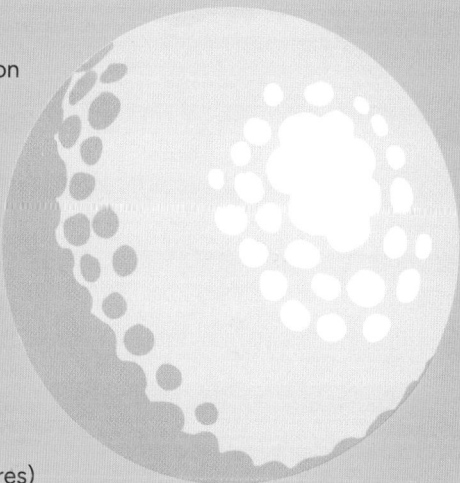

ALLAN ROBERTSON
(SCOTLAND)

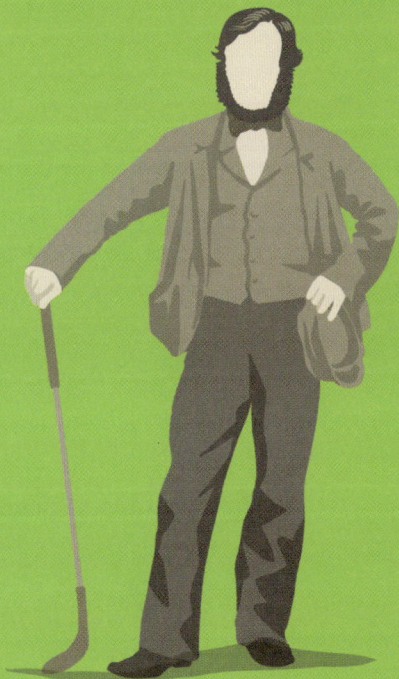

Allan Robertson was one of the greatest golfers of his generation, building a phenomenal reputation across Scotland in the early- to mid-19th century. But he did more than just play the game: he designed courses, built clubs and produced feathery balls of the very highest quality. Having the 'Allan' stamp on a feathery was a recognised sign of quality, and they are still coveted by collectors today. One came up for auction in 2007 and sold for nearly £8,000, although one made by William Robertson, Allan's father, went under the hammer for £24,000 three years previously. Either way, keep your eyes peeled if you are out and about on the St Andrews links.

The Robertson family was steeped in the history of golf, and Allan is said to have been raised in a house overlooking the 18th hole of the St Andrews Old Course. His family had been producing feathery-leatheries for more than two centuries, and the quality of what they produced meant that balls stamped with his name were as expensive as an individual golf club. He is said to have produced almost 2,500 in one year, so at the peak of his career he could probably have afforded a house overlooking every hole at St Andrews.

His company struggled with the rise of the guttie in the 1850s, though; not helped by the fact that Robertson initially stood against the tide of modernity and refused to accept the potential of the guttie ball.

He remained a superlative golfer throughout it all and is recorded as being the first golfer to get around the St Andrews Old Course in less than 80. Robertson died in 1858. In 1860, the golfers of Prestwick held a competition to see who would assume his mantle of Champion Golfer. In the 165 years since, this competition has evolved into the Open Championship, one of the four major tournaments that sit at the centre of the world's golfing calendar.

The oldest and most iconic golf course in the world is the Old Course St Andrews, known as the Old Lady or even the Grand Old Lady if you are feeling very respectful (which you really always should). Regardless of its salubrious reputation, the course itself is a public golf course open to all. It is owned, along with the six other courses in St Andrews, by the St Andrews Links Trust under an act of the British Parliament.

"It took me 17 years to get 3,000 hits in baseball. It took one afternoon on the golf course."

US baseball player Hank Aaron is open about his capabilities.

⋆ THE BOGEYMAN, THE VILLAIN ⋆

The first consistent method of scoring a round of golf started to develop towards the end of the 19th century. It set out an expected course score that you could achieve if you were doing well, but scoring one over the expected score for the hole became known as a 'bogey', a word that has been retained even though the scoring system has been refined in the subsequent 125 years or so.

There are a few explanations about how 'bogey' came into use, but most agree that the name arose in Britain before being accepted in international golfing circles. One explanation is that it's derived from the word 'boggart', which is a kind of Scottish gremlin, imp or evil spirit. A boggart is the sort of thing that would derail what might otherwise have been a good day. This fits if you are playing a round and all's going well until you meet a boggart or bogey on the 14th who puts a crimp on your day.

Another version suggests that it comes from an English music hall song called 'Hush, Hush, Hush, Here Comes The Bogeyman', which included the lines: 'Here comes the Bogeyman! Don't let him come too close to you, he'll catch you if he can'. The idea of the bogeyman is likely to have come from middle English, which was spoken from the Norman Conquest of 1066 until around the 15th century and included the word *bogge* or *bugge* to mean a frightening spectre, which is exactly what scoring 1 over par is if you are an above average golfer.

In many ways, it's the same story: something a bit unsettling, a little strange in your neighbourhood. Your preferred version of the story depends on whether you are from north or south of Hadrian's Wall. If you are from further afield, just shrug and say it's from Britain.

While golfers down the years have got creative with their birdies, eagles and condors for shots that are under par, shots over par are either bogey (+1), double bogey (+2), triple bogey (+3), and so on. There was a vague movement to get double bogeys replaced with the word 'buzzard', but it never really caught on.

Despite all the despondency surrounding bogeys from the outside, for most average golfers, getting a bogey on a hole is a perfectly acceptable score, because you are literally only one shot worse than the average. Do that 18 times in a round of golf and you'll score 90 on a par-72 course, which is something to build on for sure, but not something to be upset about.

★ THE OPEN TROPHY ★

The Open Championship was set up to honour Allan Robertson, so there's a certain propriety to it being won four out of the first eight years by his former apprentice, Old Tom Morris. Old Tom Morris won it for the final time in 1867 before his son, the imaginatively named Young Tom Morris, won the tournament in its 9th, 10th and 11th years.

The winner of the Open was originally awarded the Challenge Belt. This was pretty much a boxing belt that the winner was allowed to keep for the year until the next winner was crowned (or belted). The belt, which cost £25 to create at the time, was donated by the Earl of Eglinton, who was, by all accounts, a bit of an admirer of medieval pageantry and thought that a belt was the right way to honour the best golfer in the land.

In honour of the feat of winning the belt on three consecutive occasions, Young Tom Morris was permitted to keep it, and so a new trophy had to be developed. Despite the competition rules stating very clearly when they were first written up that anyone who won the belt three consecutive times would be allowed to keep it, and despite the fact that Young Tom Morris had won the belt in 1868 and 1869, nobody appeared to be prepared for the third consecutive victory in 1870.

As there was no trophy available, the Open wasn't held in 1871. One assumes that the sponsors wouldn't let anyone get away with that these days ... The Open has taken place every year since, with the exception of pauses for the World Wars and the Covid-19 pandemic.

To be fair to the golfing powers that be, they rectified the situation in 1872, creating the Golf Champion Trophy in the form of a grand silver claret jug, a replica of which is still awarded to this day. Young Tom Morris won it that year as well, but the trophy wasn't actually ready, so it wasn't until 1873 when it was presented for the first time to that year's victor, Tom Kidd.

In 1927, the decision was made that the original Claret Jug should be kept on display at St Andrews, with the winner subsequently being allowed to keep a replica for a year. They are also given a three-quarter sized replica to keep, as well as a medal.

The success of the British Open, which is theoretically open to all, hence the name, led to several other golfing competitions around the world adopting a similar format. The one held in Britain defines itself as the original and, as a result, is only ever known as the Open. Let the others clarify where they are held, this is the one with the Claret Jug.

There are rumours that the engravers on the Open's Claret Jug start their work before the final shot is played because they can foresee who is going to win the trophy. It is said that they only once came a cropper: in 1999, when Jean van de Velde squandered a three-shot lead as he reached the 18th at Carnoustie.

Both of these alleged facts are untrue; the engravers are simply very quick at their art, calmly taking an estimated eight seconds per letter to engrave a new name onto the trophy once they've received a little white envelope with the name on from the competition's organisers. This might mean that Ernie Els received the trophy a little quicker than Francesco Molinari, but not by much.

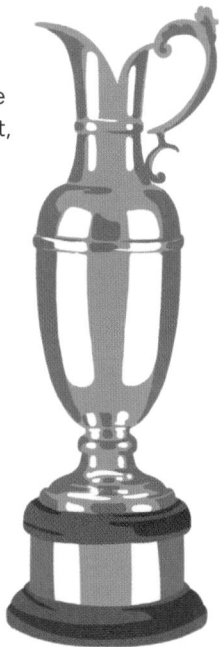

"Mistakes are part of the game. It's how well you recover from them, that's the mark of a great player."

Shock-rocker Alice Cooper, a man who spent an awful lot of the 1970s and 1980s making catastrophic mistakes, has become a keen golfer.

Golfer	Country	Total
Rory McIlroy (2011–present)	Northern Ireland	5
John Henry Taylor (1894–1913)	England	5
Byron Nelson (1937–1945)	United States	5
Peter Thomson (1954–1965)	Australia	5
Seve Ballesteros (1979–1988)	Spain	5
Brooks Koepka (2017–2023)	United States	5
Lee Trevino (1968–1984)	United States	6
Nick Faldo (1987–1996)	England	6
Phil Mickelson (2004–2021)	United States	6
Harry Vardon (1896–1914)	Jersey	7
Bobby Jones (1923–1930)	United States	7
Gene Sarazen (1922–1935)	United States	7
Sam Snead (1942–1954)	United States	7
Arnold Palmer (1958–1964)	United States	7
Tom Watson (1975–1983)	United States	8
Ben Hogan (1946–1953)	United States	9
Gary Player (1959–1978)	South Africa	9
Walter Hagen (1914–1929)	United States	11
Tiger Woods (1997–2019)	United States	15
Jack Nicklaus (1962–1986)	United States	18

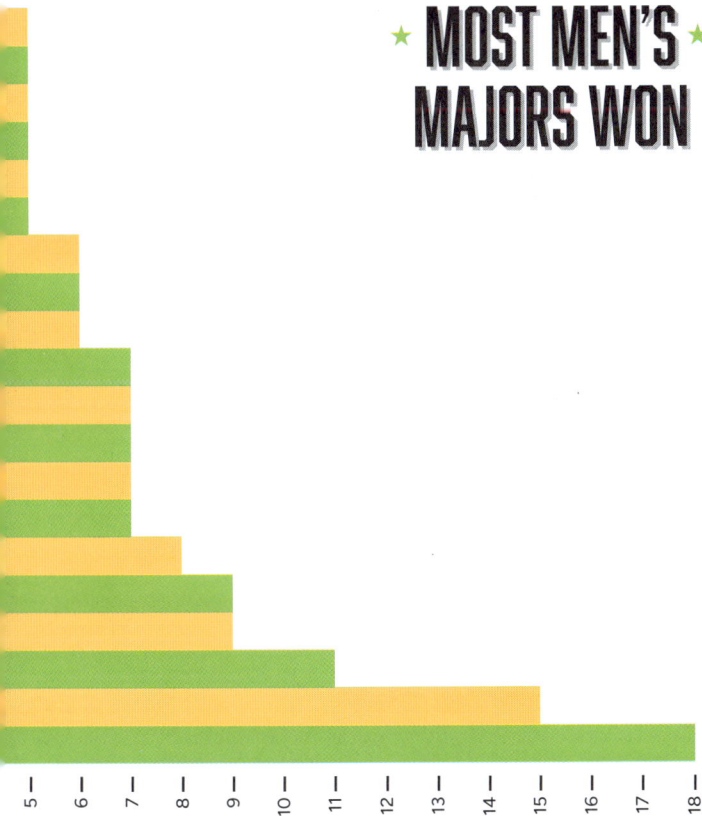

★ MOST MEN'S ★ MAJORS WON

| 5 | 6 | 7 | 8 | 9 | 10 | 11 | 12 | 13 | 14 | 15 | 16 | 17 | 18 |

OLD TOM MORRIS
(SCOTLAND)

Open Champion Old Tom Morris, father of Open Champion Young Tom Morris, had a hand in designing around 75 golf courses across the British Isles. Basically, if you stick a pin in the map of mainland Scotland, you are probably never less than 10 miles from an Old Tom Morris course.

He's basically the father of British golf, learning his trade from Allan Robertson at St Andrews before striking out on his own and building up Prestwick Golf Club. He struck the first ever ball at the Open, which he won in 1861, 1862, 1864 and 1867, narrowly avoiding being given the Prize Belt for winning it in three successive years. He left that honour to his son (see page 40).

Morris won the 1862 Open by 13 strokes, setting a record for the largest margin of victory in a major championship that stood until 2000 when the US Open was won by 15 strokes by Tiger Woods.

Morris learned his way around the golf club at St Andrews, caddying and apprenticing for Robertson; over the years, the pair developed a very successful golfing partnership, although they did have a falling out in 1848 over the new-fangled guttie ball (see page 146). He left for Prestwick in 1851 but returned to St Andrews as Keeper of the Green in 1864, after Robertson's death, carrying out extensive work to make the course fit for the rigours of late-19th century golf.

At 46 years and 99 days, Old Tom Morris remains the oldest winner of the Open. Satisfyingly, Young Tom Morris is still the tournament's youngest winner at 17 years and 156 days. The only concerning thing about this is that Tiger Woods' son is emerging as a handy golfer. Could the oldest/youngest combo become another Woods record?

Prestwick is a little south of Glasgow on the west Coast of Scotland. The club has only had seven professionals since Tom Morris went back to St Andrews in 1864. A place where people want to play and stay.

"If profanity had an influence on the flight of the ball, the game of golf would be played far better than it is."

Golfer and sportswriter Horace Hutchinson's observation should make most of us all hang our heads and mutter 'Sorry Sir'.

⭐ AFORE HISTORY ⭐

The reason why golfers shout 'Fore!' before taking a shot off the tee is fairly simple: golf balls travel a long way very fast — and if you are hit by one going at speed you'll know about it. Basically, giving some warning that a little dimpled missile is about to be unleashed is simply the polite thing to do.

The reason why the word 'fore' is used is, unfortunately, lost to history; as a result, several tales are told; some involving a nudge and a wink, and some involving some mighty French cannon (still others involve both a mighty French cannon and a nudge and a wink).

The most likely explanation, though, is relatively prosaic. Back in the day, hairy and feathery balls were expensive (see page 15). To cut down on lost balls, players often employed forecaddies to go up the fairway and keep an eye out for where the ball dropped. Players would then shout 'Forecaddie!' to warn them when a ball was about to be played, which, in the nature of things, was shortened to 'Fore!'

This may be the least exciting explanation, but it's a sad fact of life that the least exciting version of events is often the most likely.

"Life is not fair, so why should I make a course that is fair?"

Legendary course architect Pete Dye sums up the philosophy of course design that most of us suspected all along.

KO JIN-YOUNG
(KOREA)

Ko Jin-young has only just turned 30, but she's already won 15 times on the Ladies Professional Golf Association (LPGA) Tour. This haul includes two majors, the Chevron Championship and the Evian Championship. Both of these were won in 2019, the same year that she played 114 consecutive holes without a bogey, breaking a record set by Tiger Woods (110 holes, in 2000). Annoyingly, her run was broken when she missed a 90cm putt.

She continued to rewrite the record book in 2021/22 when she delivered 14 consecutive rounds where her number of strokes was in the 60s and 34 consecutive rounds below par. She's also come second at the US Women's Open and the Women's British Open.

Ko is one of a remarkable generation of South Korean players who were inspired to play golf by the exploits of Se-Ri Pak, who won the US Women's Open in 1998.

After a challenging couple of years, Ko has gone through the laborious process of reconstructing her swing and enhancing her stamina. She was joint second in the 2024 Women's PGA Championship, only three strokes off the lead, so things seem to be heading in the right direction.

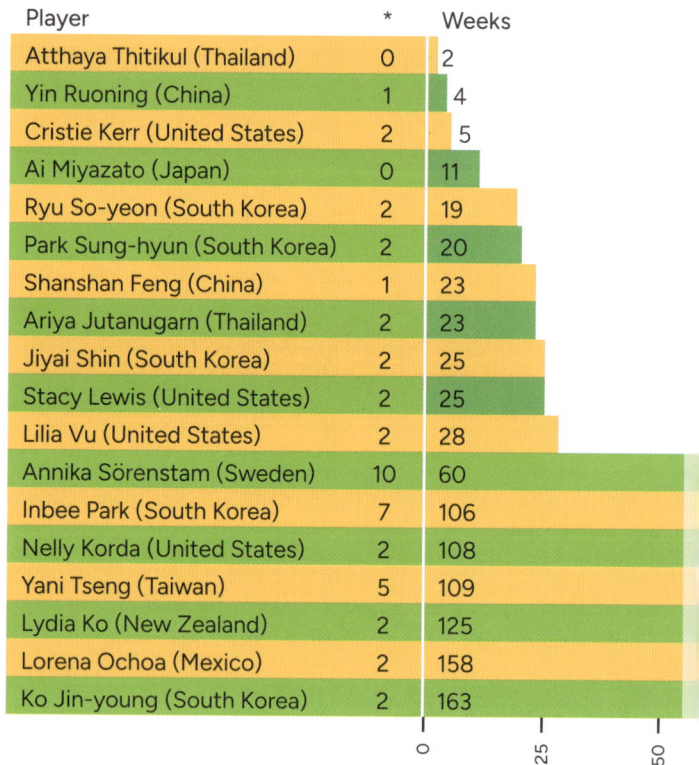

Player	*	Weeks
Atthaya Thitikul (Thailand)	0	2
Yin Ruoning (China)	1	4
Cristie Kerr (United States)	2	5
Ai Miyazato (Japan)	0	11
Ryu So-yeon (South Korea)	2	19
Park Sung-hyun (South Korea)	2	20
Shanshan Feng (China)	1	23
Ariya Jutanugarn (Thailand)	2	23
Jiyai Shin (South Korea)	2	25
Stacy Lewis (United States)	2	25
Lilia Vu (United States)	2	28
Annika Sörenstam (Sweden)	10	60
Inbee Park (South Korea)	7	106
Nelly Korda (United States)	2	108
Yani Tseng (Taiwan)	5	109
Lydia Ko (New Zealand)	2	125
Lorena Ochoa (Mexico)	2	158
Ko Jin-young (South Korea)	2	163

0   25   50

★ WEEKS AS GOLF'S ★
NUMBER ONE FEMALE PLAYER

*number of majors

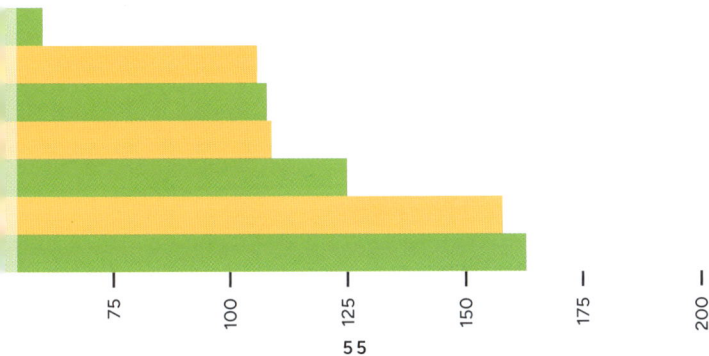

75 100 125 150 175 200

★ SANDY LYLE ★
(SCOTLAND)

Sandy Lyle was one of the biggest names in British golf in the 1980s, winning both the Open Championship, in 1985, and the Masters, in 1988. He amassed 30 professional wins, including 18 on the European Tour and six on the PGA circuit. Along with England's Nick Faldo and Wales's Ian Woosnam, he formed a triumvirate of British golfers who drove each other to higher achievements.

Although he played for Scotland, Lyle was actually born in England – his father had moved south of the border to become the professional at a golf course in Shropshire. His dad's role meant that the family lived close to the course's 18th hole; as a result, Lyle was on the course from the age of three.

Lyle's victory in the Open in 1985 was the first time that the Claret Jug had been lifted by a Brit since England's Tony Jacklin in 1969, and the first time it had been won by a Scot since George Duncan in 1920. Two years later he became the first European to win the Players Championship since it was first contested in 1974 and then the first Briton to win the Masters in 1988 (it was then won for the next two years by Nick Faldo and then Ian Woosnam took the trophy the year after that, marking a remarkable four years for golfers from these sceptred isles).

★ PREMIUM ★ PARAPHERNALIA PARADOX

There's a paradox at the heart of golf. You pay for a round of 18 holes and your target is to complete those holes with as few strokes as possible. If you really get into the sport, you also fork out for the very best tools that your disposable income will allow: you upgrade your clubs, you spend more on the best possible balls. Each of these upgrades will help you hit the ball further or putt with more precision.

The more you upgrade your kit, the fewer strokes it takes you to get around a course and the quicker you are back at the clubhouse. So, the weird thing is that the more you spend, the less value for money the whole thing is.

Cogitate on that as you contemplate buying a new driver ...

"Cow pasture pool."

American sportswriter OK Brand offers a simple description of golf.

★ ANNIKA SÖRENSTAM ★
(SWEDEN)

Annika Sörenstam won 97 professional golf tournaments, 10 of them majors, between turning professional in 1992 and retiring from competitions in 2008. She was the LPGA's Player of the Year eight times, including five consecutive awards between 2001 and 2005.

She won four of the five women's majors, specifically the US Women's Open in 1995, 1996 and 2006, the Chevron Championship in 2001, 2002 and 2005, the Women's PGA Championship in 2003, 2004 and 2005 and the Women's British Open in 2003. The only title that is missing from the career Grand Slam is the Canadian Women's Open (then known as the du Maurier Classic), although she did come second in 1998.

Second in any golfing competition is an impressive achievement, but to put Sörenstam's dominance in the women's competition into context, in addition to her 72 wins on the LPGA Tour, she also came second 46 times and third 24 times. Basically, she finished in the top three in 46% of her career LPGA starts. She also finished in the top 10 209 times overall, which is 67% of her career starts. She enjoyed the most LPGA wins of any player in both the 1990s and the 2000s.

In 2015, Sörenstam was one of seven women invited to become honorary members of The Royal and Ancient Golf Club of St

Andrews as the club moved to extend golf's reach across the female half of the population.

The Canadian Open tournament started as La Canadienne in 1973, and became a major in 1979, holding the accolade until 2001. Pat Bradley holds the record for the most victories as a major with three, although Meg Mallon and Lydia Ko have subsequently also won it three times, twice as an amateur in Ko's case.

"I regard golf as an expensive way of playing marbles,"

explains author and philosopher G.K. Chesterton. Most players have lost their marbles on one course or another.

Players	Country	Caps
Brittany Lincicome (2007–2017)	USA	6
Dottie Pepper (1990–2000)	USA	6
Morgan Pressel (2007–2019)	USA	6
Kelly Robbins (1994–2003)	USA	6
Angela Stanford (2003–2015)	USA	6
Liselotte Neumann (1990–2000)	Sweden	6
Alison Nicholas (1990–2000)	England	6
Paula Creamer (2005–2017)	USA	7
Rosie Jones (1990–2005)	USA	7
Lexi Thompson (2013–2024)	USA	7
Carlota Ciganda (2013–2024)	Spain	7
Charley Hull (2013–2023)	England	7
Beth Daniel (1990–2005)	USA	8
Meg Mallon (1992–2005)	USA	8
Helen Alfredsson (1990–2009)	Sweden	8
Sophie Gustafson (1998–2011)	Sweden	8
Trish Johnson (1990–2007)	England	8
Annika Sörenstam (1994–2007)	Sweden	8
Juli Inkster (1992–2011)	USA	9
Cristie Kerr (2002–2017)	USA	9
Catriona Matthew (1998–2017)	Scotland	9
Suzann Pettersen (2002–2019)	Norway	9
Anna Nordqvist (2009–2024)	Sweden	9
Laura Davies (1990–2011)	England	12

★ MOST-CAPPED ★
SOLHEIM CUP PLAYERS

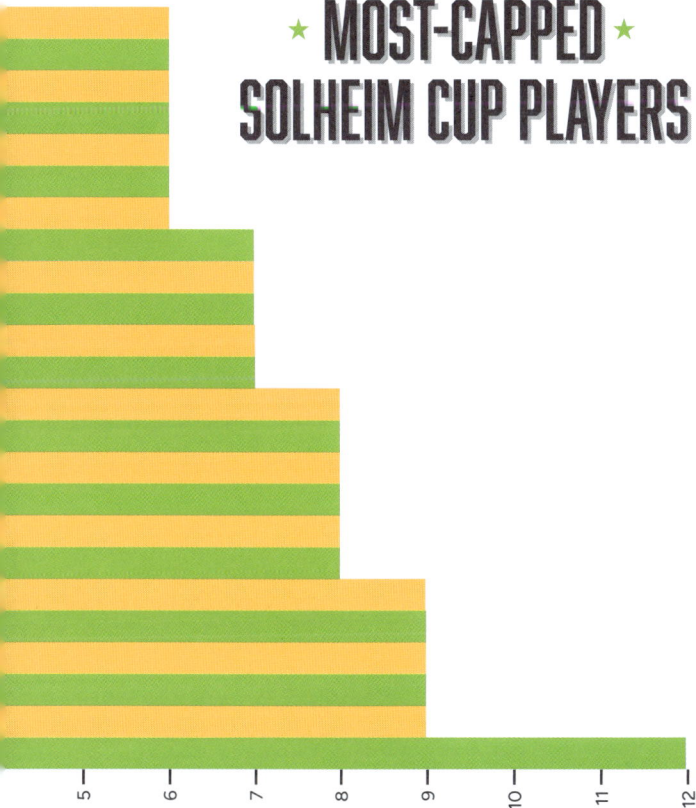

5   6   7   8   9   10   11   12

★ GENTLEMEN ONLY, ★ LADIES FORBIDDEN?

Golf has something of a reputation for being a somewhat exclusively male sport, which is not necessarily always completely fair. It's also not necessarily always completely unfair, but ... shall we just say it's nuanced and get on with it?

We know that Mary, Queen of Scots, who ruled Scotland as much as anyone between 1542 and 1567, was a keen player of the game, and it is suggested that she might have commissioned the original links course at St Andrews. Golf may have been responsible for her ultimate fall from grace, as she was observed having a round within days of her husband's suspicious death – suspicious in that the room underneath his bedroom was filled with gunpowder and exploded while he was in bed. From what CSI: Middle Ages Scotland could tell, he'd also been strangled before the explosion.

The first recorded golf tournament for women took place just down the road from St Andrews in Musselburgh in 1811. First prize was said to be a handsome wicker basket and a shawl, great for keeping off those wee hoolies from the Firth, while second and third place took home a fine pair of silk handkerchiefs from Barcelona. Which is nice. To be fair, playing for items of clothing was fairly standard at the time: When Allan Robertson (see page 34) beat Old Tom Morris (see page 46) in what is thought to be one of the only times that the pair played competitively, the prize was a jacket.

The St Andrews Ladies Golf Club was formed in 1867, with a rising number of female players across Britain joining various generally women-only clubs throughout the next few years. Across the Atlantic, the first known women's club was formed in 1891 in the New York area, while the first golfing tournament held in Australia was a women's event held in 1894.

So, the popularity of the women's game accelerated around the world at around the same time as the men's game, and while women's clubs and courses and competitions tended to be kept at arm's length from the men's set-up, golf's authorities didn't go out of their way to stop women playing.

The LPGA was set up in 1950 by 13 women who wanted to create the opportunity for the best female players to compete – and for them to be seen to be competing. The creation of the Solheim Cup, brainchild of Karsten Solheim (founder of equipment manufacturer PING), built on this foundation from 1990, creating an equivalent of the men's Ryder Cup that put women's golf in front of a global audience of millions.

There are currently five major championships in women's golf, including one in France. They started being formally recognised in the 1930s, and for the first 60 years they were absolutely dominated by US players. More recently, players from South Korea, Sweden and Australia have started to make their presence felt.

The French Open – or the Open de France Dames to be precise – has been played every year since 1987, except for 1990, 1991, 1992 and 1998. Held historically at various clubs, in 2022 it made history when Ines Laklalech was the first Moroccan, Arab and North African player to win a Ladies European Tour title.

"Golf ... is the infallible test. The man who can go into a patch of rough alone, with the knowledge that only God is watching him, and play his ball where it lies, is the man who will serve you faithfully and well,"

suggests P.G. Wodehouse. The only problem with that is that if no one is watching, how can you tell if they decide to cheat?

★ PHIL MICKELSON ★
(USA)

Phil Mickelson very nearly had a very satisfyingly neat set of major tournament results: he won the Open Championship once (2013), the PGA Championship twice (2005, 2021), the Masters three times (2004, 2006, 2010) but then ruined it all by only coming second in the US Open. That said, he came second six times (1999, 2002, 2004, 2006, 2009, 2013), which is a phenomenal achievement.

The good thing is, though, that he could still neaten it all up; despite the fact that he turned professional in 1992, he shows little inclination to retire, with his 2021 PGA Championship victory making him the oldest winner of a major tournament in golf. The only wrinkle is that Mickelson has become a vocal supporter of the LIV golf tournament, which might stand in the way of a career Grand Slam. From his perspective, the sacrifice might be worth it as he stands up for players' rights, as he perceives them.

An odd thing that's often talked about is that he's a naturally right-handed person but plays left-handed because he learned to play by mirroring his right-handed father's swing at an early age.

★ STROKES: IS THIS IT? ★

The thing with vocabulary is that while it can seem like it's there to complicate, it's often there to simplify. Take the word 'stroke'. A stroke in golf is a single thing that can cover several activities, such as a drive, a putt, a pitch or even a complete miss (sometimes called a 'whiff'). When it comes to totting up the scores, though, it doesn't matter which specific activity you did; all that matters is whether you played a stroke and how many strokes it took you to complete the hole.

How you got there, the good and bad decisions you made, the right and wrong clubs you used – they only matter when it comes to the story of the round, and that only matters when you are telling a yarn about it later. The winning and the losing, the birdies, the eagles and the bogies, that's all down to the strokes.

But why is it called a stroke rather than, for example, a swing, which would more accurately reflect the motion that the player makes when they address the ball? It all comes down to the scoring. Each swing would be marked on a score card with the stroke of a pencil, and, given that the number of strokes was all-important, all the drives, putts, pitches and complete misses simply became known as a stroke.

'Golf is so popular simply because it is the best game in the world at which to be bad,"

said A.A. Milne. Sometimes you are Tigger on the golf course, sometimes you are Eeyore, and sometimes you are just Pooh.

★ WATCH THE BIRDIE ★

Golf has developed its own language down the years, and 'birdie' is one of those words that people use without really knowing where it comes from. In some ways, it doesn't matter because if you know what it means then you are perfectly entitled to use it.

But you're here because you want to expand your knowledge (or you want something to do on in a quiet moment other than look at your phone), so here's the probable root of the word 'birdie' in golfing terms … Back at the turn of the 20th century, people in the US who were expressing their appreciation of something would say: "It was the bird." So, if you made a good shot, you might say: "That was a bird of a shot."

The story goes that the player who made that first bird of a shot was playing for a bit of money per hole and suggested that they double the money if the winner of a hole got a score of 1-under par. The other players agreed and a tradition was born.

Its first recorded use is said to have been at the Atlantic City Country Club in 1903, or possibly earlier, depending on which history you read. The Atlantic City Country Club has a little plaque stating that it happened in 1903, and who are we to argue? Either way, the word slowly evolved and by 1910, 'birdie' had become a standard bit of golfing slang for a nice shot, particularly in the US.

Now, you might think that our great-great-grandparents saying something is "the bird" when they mean that it's good sounds a little strange, but that's the nature of slang. If the word were invented today, when the kids are constantly saying that things are 'sick', we'd have ended up with 'sickie' instead of 'birdie', so in a lot of ways we've got off lightly.

Brian Harman has scored the most career birdies in PGA tour history with 4,592 over 455 events. In the women's tournaments, Beth Daniel and Amy Yang have the most consecutive LPGA birdies on record – nine in a row.

"If you want to hit it further, hit it better."

With pro tips like that, one hates to think how much Jack Nicklaus charged for professional lessons.

★ EAGLE ON THE 9TH ★

Birdies are cool and all, and for many players, getting a birdie is just the sort of thing that makes your day, but what's better than a birdie? What would give you the right to swagger into the clubhouse and receive the instant respect of everyone there? Bigger wingspan, more majestic?

It's an eagle – achieved when you take two shots less than the hole's par score.

From there, things can get a little convoluted: An eagle putt is a putt that finds the hole and saves the golfer two shots. For example, if you are on a par-5, reach the green in two and then find the pin in a single putt, you've made an eagle-putt.

But on a par-3, you could also find the pin with a single shot, which is a form of eagle known as a 'hole in one', which is so self-explanatory that we won't bother to go into it here (although we do on page 98). If you swagger into the clubhouse and lead with the fact that you scored an eagle rather than a hole in one people will be impressed, but it's probably better just to lead with the hole in one. It's like playing poker and laying down two pair and two pair rather than saying you've got four of a kind: Cut to the chase, take the kudos and get your round in.

Player	Country	Wins
Cary Middlecoff (1945–1961)	United States	39
Tom Watson (1974–1998)	United States	39
Walter Hagen (1914–1936)	United States	45
Phil Mickelson (1991–2021)	United States	45
Billy Casper (1956–1975)	United States	51
Byron Nelson (1935–1951)	United States	52
Arnold Palmer (1955–1973)	United States	62
Ben Hogan (1938–1959)	United States	64
Jack Nicklaus (1962–1986)	United States	73
Sam Snead (1936–1965)	United States	82
Tiger Woods (1996–2019)	United States	82

0   10   15

★ MOST MEN'S ★ PGA TOURS WON

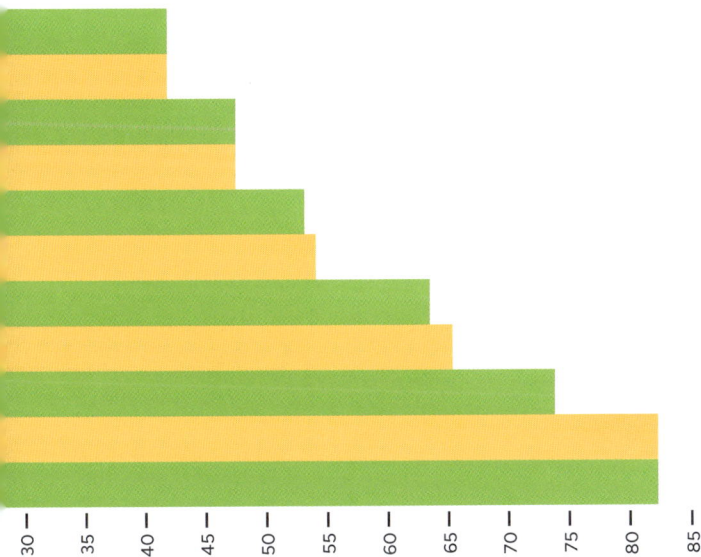

| 30 | 35 | 40 | 45 | 50 | 55 | 60 | 65 | 70 | 75 | 80 | 85 |

★ RORY McILROY ★
(NORTHERN IRELAND)

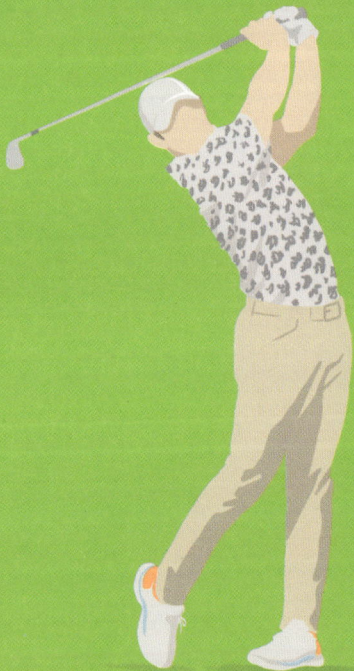

Rory McIlroy came to the fore when he took his first European Tour victory in 2009, adding a PGA Tour victory a year later. He subsequently won the US Open Championship in 2011, the PGA Championship in 2012 and 2014 and the Open Championship in 2014.

It was another 11 years before he finally completed the career Grand Slam by winning the Masters. He'd come second in 2022, and while this was rightly recognised as a significant achievement, it wasn't quite *the* achievement. Finally though, to the delight of virtually every golf fan and probably a decent majority of professional players, his day arrived in April 2025 in Augusta, and he became only the sixth player, and the first European, to achieve a career Grand Slam.

He's chalked up 44 professional wins so far in his career, but possibly the highlight (at least for those of us with internet access) is being able to watch a 9-year-old McIlroy chip a golf ball into a washing machine on a Northern Irish television talk show. Apparently, he used to use the washing machine a lot as part of his training regime, so they got him to give a demonstration on television. He was not rinsed.

★ STAY HERE AND LISTEN TO ★ THE NIGHTMARE OF THE GREEN

After the eagle comes the albatross, a beautiful bird that is very rarely seen over land. Which makes it perfect for a shot that's 3-under par. It's not impossible – it does happen, but it's big and very rare.

If you think about it, it's actually rarer than a hole in one, because basically you need to get though a par-5 fairway in two shots and then take a single putt to sink the ball. Which is quite a feat given that par-5s are recommended to be 450–710 yards (410–650 metres) for men and 370–600 yards (340–550 metres) for women.

Not impossible, but unusual.

Some people also call an albatross a 'double eagle', in the same way a bogey is 1-over par and a double bogey is two over. There's no issue with this; if they want to use two words when one will suffice, that's fine. Perhaps they are paid by the word rather than the simplicity of the concepts that they are trying to put across. Lawyers, in other words.

"It's not whether you win or lose – but whether I win or lose,"

observes gentleman golfer Sandy Lyle.

★ UNDER PAR, OVER PAR ... ★

The origins of the par system stretch back to the late 19th century. Prior to that, golf had been played against the people who you were with and that was about it. You came off the course with a score – you'd done well, you'd done not so well – you went about your day.

The word 'par' is originally Latin and simply means 'average'. The way that it is used in golf is probably borrowed from the stock exchanges, where the value of a stock would be described as above or below par according to its perceived market value. In 1870, a golf writer was talking to a couple of professionals about what a winning score in the Open on the Prestwick course would be, and when he got his answer, he reported it as 'par for the course'.

At this point there was just a phrase.

It wasn't until 1911 that the United States Golf Association (USGA) made the term official by setting out recommended course lengths and difficulties. The current USGA definition of par is: "the score that an expert player would be expected to make for a given hole. Par means expert play under ordinary weather conditions, allowing two strokes on the putting green." This means that you should only really be shooting anywhere near a par if you are an expert golfer. The rest of us might achieve it on the odd hole here and there, but not across an entire round.

Basically, par is something to aim for.

There have only been 18 albatrosses scored in men's Majors, with the first being scored by Gene Sarazen at Augusta in 1935, and the latest by Joey Sindelar in 2006. They are even rarer in women's tournaments – just five have been scored, most recently by Lui Yan at the 2025 Chevron Championship.

★ US/WORLD PAR SCORES THROUGH THE YEARS ★

Par 5 +18% ▬▬▬
Par 4 + 15% ▬▬▬
Par 3 + 9% ▬▬▬

Yards

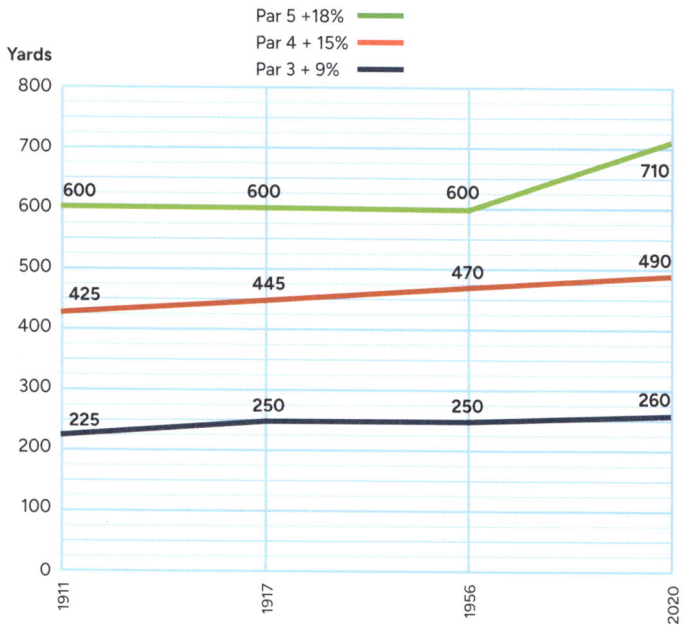

THE AVERAGE SIZE OF THE PRIZE
(1990-2024)

Average men's winnings

Average women's winnings

$

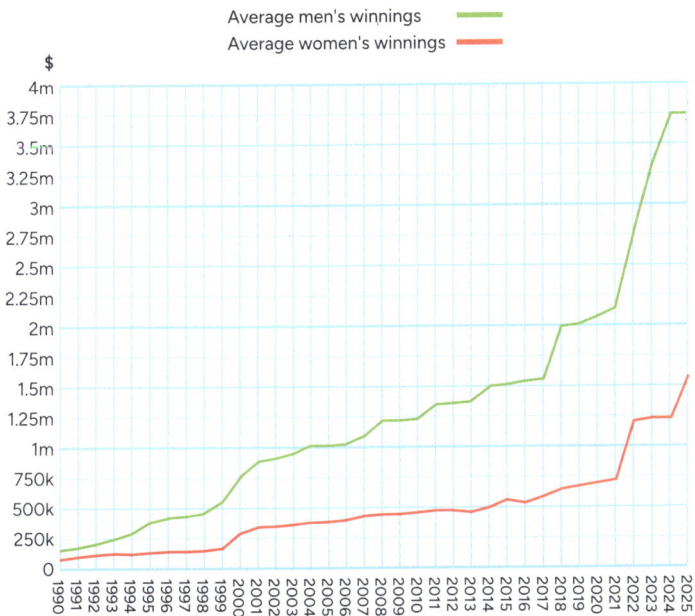

"It is more satisfying to be a bad player at golf. The worse you play, the better you remember the occasional good shot."

Nubar Gulbenkian, noted Armenian-British business magnate and socialite, makes a point that gives us all hope.

⭐ TRIPLE CROWNS ⭐ AND GRAND SLAMS

Albatrosses are not the only things in golf that are very rare. There are four men's major golf championships (also known as 'the major championships', furthermore known as 'the majors'), and if you win three of them in the same year, you have won golf's Triple Crown. Win all four and you've got yourself a Grand Slam.

The Triple Crown has only been achieved twice in modern golfing history. In 1953, Ben Hogan won the Masters, the US Open and the Open Championship, earning himself a ticker-tape parade in New York for his troubles.

Tiger Woods (who else?) delivered the second Triple Crown in 2000, winning the US Open, the Open and the PGA Championship. He doesn't seem to have had a ticker-tape parade, so there are some honours that have eluded him, although to be fair to Woods, New York has cut right back on its ticker-tape parades since the 1960s. Might be something to do with the fact that ticker-tape machines, which provided stock market information to traders back in the day, are not really used any more.

Grand Slams are even rarer than Triple Crowns, with only one recorded in the history of golf. In 1930, Bobby Jones won all four majors, and was also honoured by a ticker-tape parade in New York. It was actually his second time being showered with ticker-tape; the first was in 1926 when he became the first American to win the Open.

To be fair to Hogan, he might have been able to turn his 1953 Triple Crown into a Grand Slam but for a quirk of the calendar which meant that the PGA Championship overlapped with qualifying for the Open.

Also to be fair to Woods, he did win four consecutive majors – three in 2000 and the first major of 2001 – so, if you squint at it, he's kind of won a Grand Slam.

Gene Sarazen, Ben Hogan, Gary Player, Jack Nicklaus and Tiger Woods have all won a career Grand Slam, which is not to be sniffed at.

Australia and South Africa both have domestic Triple Crowns.

"A shot that goes in the cup is pure luck, but a shot to within two feet of the flag is skill."

Ben Hogan has gone down in golfing history as the man who invented practising so he's worth listening to.

Player	Country	Wins
Susie Berning (1965–1973)	United States	4
Donna Caponi (1969–1981)	United States	4
Laura Davies (1987–1996)	England	4
Sandra Haynie (1965–1982)	United States	4
Meg Mallon (1991–2004)	United States	4
Hollis Stacy (1977–1984)	United States	4
Amy Alcott (1979–1991)	United States	5
Se-Ri Pak (1998–2006)	South Korea	5
Yani Tseng (2008–2011)	Taiwan	5
Pat Bradley (1980–1986)	United States	6
Betsy King (1987–1997)	United States	6
Patty Sheehan (1983–1996)	United States	6
Kathy Whitworth (1965–1975)	United States	6
Juli Inkster (1984–2002)	United States	7
Karrie Webb (1999–2006)	Australia	7
Inbee Park (2008–2015)	South Korea	7
Betsy Rawls (1951–1969)	United States	8
Annika Sörenstam (1995–2006)	Sweden	10
Babe Zaharias (1940–1954)	United States	10
Louise Suggs (1946–1959)	United States	11
Mickey Wright (1958–1966)	United States	13
Patty Berg (1937–1958)	United States	15

★ MOST WOMEN'S ★ MAJORS WON

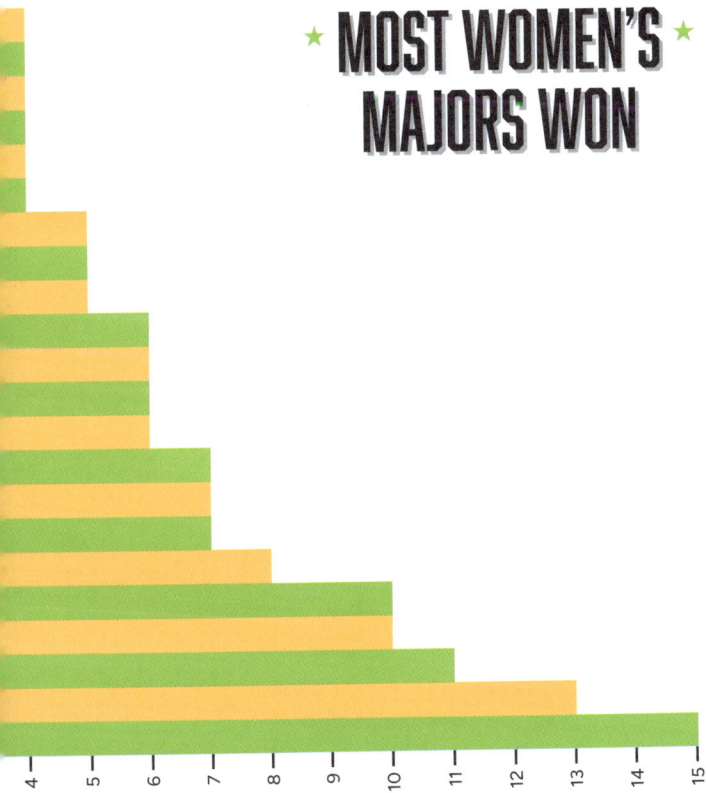

4 5 6 7 8 9 10 11 12 13 14 15

ARNOLD PALMER

(USA)

With the arrival of television coverage in the 1950s and 60s, golf moved from being the preserve of the country club set and into mainstream America – and Arnold Palmer, former US Coast Guard and paint salesman, became one of its everyman stars.

Palmer's run on the Open Championship – second in 1960, winning in 1961 and 1962 – is said to have put the British tournament back on the agenda for American players, who had slightly drawn back from it in recent years, partly because it was a long way to travel at the dawn of the jet age, and particularly given that the prize pot was relatively modest.

Palmer also dominated the Masters during the period, winning it in 1958, 1960, 1962 and 1964, coming third in 1959 and joint second in 1961 (alongside Charles Coe) and 1965 (alongside Gary Player). In all, he took part in 50 consecutive Masters tournaments, completing his final one in 2004.

He also won the US Open in 1960 and was a runner-up in the PGA Championship in 1964, 1968 and 1970.

Palmer was very much part of the zeitgeist in the 1960s, even being namechecked in *Goldfinger*, the 1964 adaptation of the 1957 James Bond book of the same name, with Bond's caddie commenting: "If that's [Goldfinger's] original ball, I'm

Arnold Palmer" during a friendly/big man posturing game of golf between the protagonist and the rarely very secret agent. Goldfinger got his just desserts for cheating later in the film, even though it was technically Bond that cheated more egregiously in the golf …

Palmer, meanwhile, apparently liked to keep up with the game he loved, and one of the ways that he did this was to send letters to players who had just won tournaments around the world. One such letter is said to have been sent to Rory McIlroy after he'd won the 2011 US Open and contained the advice: "Just continue to be yourself." There are no better words of wisdom.

To make the ultimate summertime refresher, an Arnold Palmer mocktail, mix ½ a cup of lemonade with ¼ cup of iced tea. Pour both ingredients into a tall glass filled with ice and mix. Garnish with a slice of lemon. The drink is named after Palmer, who often requested this drink.

"Why am I using a new putter? Because the last one didn't float too well."

Professional golfer
Craig Stadler.

★ IT'S JUST WHAT HAPPENS ★ IF YOU GIVE AN INFINITE NUMBER OF MONKEYS AN INFINITE NUMBER OF TYPEWRITERS ...

The history of the term 'hole in one' really, really isn't deep. Through a mixture of experience, knowledge, practice and absolute luck, it is possible to hit a ball off the tee and into the hole. It's very rare, but it *is* possible.

The long and the short of it is that golf holes are very small, golf balls are fractionally smaller and a fairway is really big (relatively). This means it's exceedingly rare to strike a ball from the tee and for it to drop obligingly into a hole. On the other side of the equation, though, hundreds of people strike the ball off the tee each week, so sometimes one of them will do the seemingly impossible and sink the ball on the first shot.

This is golf, so someone, somewhere has crunched the numbers and come to the conclusion that a hole in one will be scored on average every 3,125 rounds of golf played. For an amateur golfer, there's a hole in one waiting every 12,500 times they step up to the tee. Encouragingly, this means that an amateur should score a hole in one once every 194 rounds, meaning that if they play a single round of golf every week, they are almost guaranteed to enjoy a hole in one every four years. Because that's exactly how maths works.

For the professional it's estimated to be more like one in 2,500, which roughly translates to a little under once a year if they play 18 holes three times per week. Of course it would be nice if it happened in an important final with the cameras watching every time, but that's really not how maths works.

The long and the short of it is that it's long odds, but not unobtainable. It's just not something you want to bet the house on.

That's the maths. From a language point of view, we really don't need to dwell on it. It's a hole in one because it has taken the player a single shot to get the ball in the hole. It's also known as an 'ace', although that tends to be used more in the US.

Old Tom Morris achieved one of the first recorded holes-in-one during the 1868 Open Championship.

There is a tradition that anyone who scores a hole in one buys a round for anyone in the 19th hole – also known as the clubhouse. This can make it an expensive achievement, particularly on a tournament day. But fear not, happy golfer, those lovely people in the risk management and insurance markets have a solution: hole-in-one insurance is available and will cover your bar bill in the event of delivering an ace.

> **The Masters is one of the greatest challenges that a golfer can take on. Despite this, 34 players have scored a hole-in-one during the championship, the first at the inaugural event in 1934 and the most recent in 2022. Since 1954, players have been awarded a large crystal bowl if they manage a hole-in-one.**

"Golf's beauty lies not in its perfection, but in the way it mirrors life's imperfections."

A philosophical Phil Mickelson reflects on how life imitates the art of golf.

★ WHAT IS GOLFER AND ★ WHAT IS EQUIPMENT?

Golf is constantly evolving, and golfing authorities are continuously having to balance the need to keep moving forward and keep encouraging people into the game with the need to make sure that the game is difficult enough to remain a challenge and is true to its original spirit.

There has always been a debate about whether golfers have got better or whether the improvements in equipment have made them better. Exclusively for this book, we can reveal the definitive answer: it's a bit of both!

Modern golfing equipment is based on a level of understanding of the universe that our ancestors could only dream of. We won't ever know everything, but we understand material sciences, aerodynamics and human anatomy in far more detail than we did even 50 years ago – and if you understand those three things, you can build better golf equipment and develop better golfers.

Balanced against that, golfing authorities have to make sure that the game does not just become a parade of high-tech gimmickry that removes the natural element of the game. We now have the technology to sit in the clubhouse and use our phones to launch round, ball-shaped drones in the direction of the hole, but would it be as fun? Would it be as regularly heartbreaking? Would it be golf?

Either way, if you compare the original US regulations for hole length from 1911 with the modern equivalents, you can see that they aren't too far apart. Par-3 has only gone up by 9%, par-4 by 15% and par-5 by 18%.

Golf is supposed to be a challenge, and getting par on any hole is an achievement for the vast majority of players. New technology and enhanced equipment is always coming into the game, so keeping it balanced with the players' skill is always going to be a struggle, but it's a struggle that gives the greenkeepers an occasional smirk.

★ LEE TREVINO ★
(USA)

Lee Trevino played with swagger, was always ready with a quip and, bizarrely, sometimes a rubber snake. He grew up poor in Texas, learning to play golf by sneaking onto courses when no one was looking in order to hit a few tired old balls with a set of clubs that had seen better days. Someone at some point seems to have accepted that the irrepressible Trevino was going to keep going there no matter what they did to discourage him, so he ended up being taken on as a caddie – and from there he hustled his way to the very top of the game.

He won 29 PGA Tour events, including the US Open twice (in 1968 and 1971), the Open Championship (in 1971 and 1972) and the PGA Championship (in 1974 and 1984). For 14 consecutive seasons, Trevino won at least one PGA Tour event, as well as a string of professional tournaments around the world.

In the middle of all these victories, in 1975, he was struck by lightning, suffering a major injury to his back. The injuries were severe enough that the hospital suggested he put a call in to his wife in case something went wrong with the operations he was going to need. Did he express his feelings, tell his wife how much she meant to him? He did not. He made a quip, which, to be fair, was probably the most reassuring thing he could have done.

The rubber snake thing comes from the first tee of an 18-hole play-off at the US Open in 1971, where Trevino was taking on Jack Nicklaus and apparently pulled a writhing snake from his golf bag rather than the expected driver. Nicklaus was deeply nonplussed but Trevino took the round by three shots, so maybe the snake worked.

Lee Trevino was not the only professional golfer to have been struck by lightning that day in 1975. Jerry Heard, standing with Trevino, was also hit and seriously injured. Tony Jacklin was holding an 8-iron when he was hit by a bolt, which knocked the club out of his hands and sent it flying 30 feet. He then watched as Bobby Nickols was knocked to the ground by a different bolt of lightning. Remarkably, they all survived.

"You don't know what pressure is until you play for five bucks with only two bucks in your pocket."

Lee Trevino.

THE SEMI-MYTHICAL CONDOR

Sometimes people give things names on principle, secure in the knowledge that they are almost never going to be used. Achieving a 4-under par shot is stupendously rare and has only been officially achieved a handful of times in golf history. Yes, everybody has met someone at the 19th hole who claims that they once achieved it, but we all know the truth.

Interestingly, both the condor and the albatross have wingspans of up to 3.5 metres, breaking the birdie to eagle to albatross size hierarchy. It's worth noting, though, that the terms are not really officially official, so no one was carefully checking their books of ornithology when they were defined.

Possibly renaming a condor a pterodactyl, which had a wingspan of up to 11 metres, might be more appropriate, but it's unlikely to catch on. Not least because pterodactyls are currently extinct, so you'll never see one except on telly, whereas condors are simply extremely rare (unless you live in the Andes or California, and the Californian ones are actually smaller than their Andean cousins ... anyway ... golf).

"I would like to deny all allegations by Bob Hope that during my last game of golf, I hit an eagle, a birdie, an elk and a moose."

Former US President Gerald Ford is forced to issue a statement about his golfing prowess.

★ THE RYDER CUP ★

The Ryder Cup has taken place every two years or so in late September or early October since 1927. In its current form, it's a competition between Europe and America, although between 1927 and 1947, Great Britain were originally America's adversaries. This was extended to include Northern Ireland in 1947, the Republic of Ireland in 1953 and then the whole of Europe in 1979.

The competition has become more evenly balanced since the Europeans joined the fun, with the Americans winning just under half the time and the Europeans winning just over. When it was just Great Britain and Northern Ireland, the US won around 85% of the time, which is probably good for the ego but not exactly competitive. To be fair to Great Britain and Ireland, their combined population is around 71 million compared to the US population of 333 million, so there was a slightly deeper pool of potential golfers to draw on across the pond. Adding the population of Europe hopefully evens the balance a bit.

The Ryder Cup sort of sprouted out of the British Open. In 1920, an American golf magazine proposed to raise a fund to send a team of US golfers over to Britain for the 1921 Open. This led to 12 golfers travelling by ship to the UK, in time to have a warm-up match against a group of British golfers at Gleneagles, which was known as the Glasgow Herald 1000 Guinea Tournament. The American golfers eventually won the 1921 Open.

In 1926, Samuel Ryder, an English seed magnate (basically the bloke who invented selling little one-penny packets of seeds to domestic gardeners – and did very well out of it – but is sadly absolutely no relation to Eurovision's Sam Ryder), sponsored the cup that ended up bearing his name, with the first competition formally known as the Ryder Cup being staged at the Worcester Country Club in Massachusetts, USA in June 1927.

Players	Country	Caps
Billy Casper (1961–1975)	USA	8
Raymond Floyd (1969–1993)	USA	8
Lanny Wadkins (1977–1993)	USA	8
Tiger Woods (1997–2018)	USA	8
Peter Alliss (1953–1969)	England	8
Seve Ballesteros (1979–1995)	Spain	8
Neil Coles (1961–1977)	England	8
Bernard Gallacher (1969–1983)	Scotland	8
Bernard Hunt (1953–1969)	England	8
Colin Montgomerie (1991–2006)	Scotland	8
Sam Torrance (1981–1995)	Scotland	8
Ian Woosnam (1983–1997)	Wales	8
Jim Furyk (1997–2014)	USA	9
Dai Rees (1937–1961)	Wales	9
Sergio García (1999–2021)	Spain	10
Bernhard Langer (1981–2002)	Germany	10
Christy O'Connor Sr (1955–1973)	Republic of Ireland	10
Nick Faldo (1977–1997)	England	11
Lee Westwood (1997–2021)	England	11
Phil Mickelson (1995–2018)	USA	12

★ MOST-CAPPED ★ RYDER CUP PLAYERS

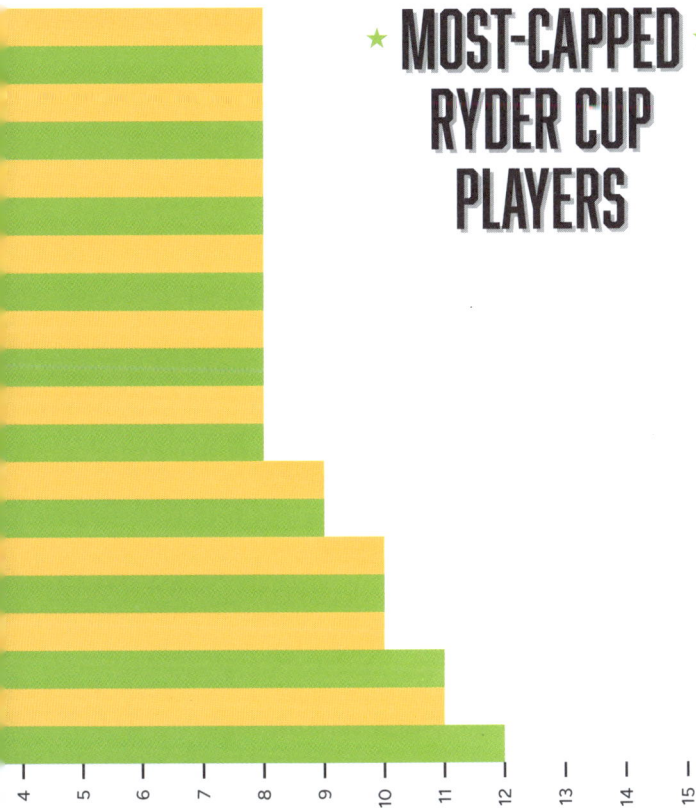

4 — 5 — 6 — 7 — 8 — 9 — 10 — 11 — 12 — 13 — 14 — 15 —

SIR NICK FALDO

(ENGLAND)

Nick Faldo was 14 when he fell in love with golf, watching Jack Nicklaus being narrowly denied victory in the 1971 Masters by a rubber snake (see page 100). Despite having never previously picked up a club, three years later Faldo was competing in amateur competitions, and a year after that he was winning them.

He turned professional in 1976, becoming the youngest person to compete in the Ryder Cup a year later, when he also won all three of his matches.

He went on to win the Masters in 1989, 1990 and 1996 and the Open in 1987, 1990 and 1992, the first British player to win the Open three times since Henry Cotton in 1934, 1937 and 1948.

Faldo captained the European Ryder Cup team in 2008 and was an early victim of the rapid improvements in camera lenses when he was pictured holding a piece of paper that gave away his plans for the next day's pairings. He tried to laugh it off as the team's lunch orders but it all turned into a bit of a brouhaha that sold a lot of newspapers but didn't really help the European performance.

★ THE GOLF CLUB ★

The first known set of specially made golf clubs was commissioned by James IV of Scotland from a bow-maker in Perth in 1502. There were quite a few bow-makers about at the time (due to the often tepid relations between most of the countries of western Europe back then), and their skills transferred neatly to making golf clubs: honing long sticks of wood into a shaft that is simultaneously sturdy and supple. The rise of the cannon and the musket at around the same time would have encouraged bow-makers to look for new sources of income.

The name of James IV's club-maker is lost to time, but we do know that the first known set had a range of clubs that would be familiar to players today. There were long-noses for driving, grassed drivers for mid-range and fairway shots, spoons and niblicks for short and chip shots, and a cleek for putting. It's all the same, only the names have changed, as a wise man once said.

All the clubs would have been made of wood. The shafts would have been made of a supple wood like hazel, while the heads, bound to the shaft by a splint and a leather strap, would have been a harder wood, such as apple or pear.

Feathery balls arrived in the early 17th century (see page 16), but they were expensive and delicate, so even though iron was available at the time, wood continued to be the main material used for clubs in those early days.

Iron started to be used sparingly for niblicks at the end of the 18th century. Then, early in the 19th century, hickory started to be imported from the US and quickly became the wood of choice for golf clubs.

It was the arrival of the contentious guttie ball (see page 18) that heralded the first major change to the configuration of the golf club. The guttie was a more solid ball, and the elegant long-nose club didn't stand up so well to repeated hits. As a result, the wooden head became more bulbous and a new class of club – the bulger – arrived.

Irons arrived a little later, around the mid-to-late 19th century, when drop-forging made them more consistent, lighter, and easier to produce and use. This was a period that saw a lot of innovation, with grooves arriving on club heads to enhance backspin and steel shafts offering durability and control.

By the mid-20th century, it wasn't uncommon for golfers to be lugging around 30 golf clubs in their bags, so the powers that be decided to limit the number of clubs that a player could carry to 14, presumably to cut down on some of the dithering that having so many options would naturally encourage. The current golf club numbering system was introduced at the same time, which in some ways is a shame because it means the word 'mashie', the original and often highly appropriate word for what is now the prosaic 5-iron, has been lost to the fairway. Not all progress is good.

That tightening of the rules was the last major change in the format of the golf club, although the emergence of computers and the arrival of new materials and composite materials has led to a lot of enhancements in the way that golf clubs perform.

There are always those who hanker for a return to a simpler age, though, and over the last few years, hickory golfing has come to prominence in many parts of the world, with players dedicated to finding and restoring old golf clubs to their former glory. They claim that hickory golf clubs give them a better feel for the club when taking a shot. The world is also full of classic car enthusiasts and people who prefer to listen to music on a gramophone. Who is to say that they are wrong?

"You know what they say about big hitters … the woods are full of them."

Jimmy Demaret, the first three-time winner of the Masters, knew that power was irrelevant without control.

★ PANTONE 342: ★
MASTERS GREEN

The Masters is one of the four major tournaments in the golfing calendar, and if you win it, you are allowed to join an elite group of golfers who are entitled to wear one of the Augusta National Golf Club's celebrated green jackets. But how did the tradition come about?

This is golf, so there are at least two stories, and the chances are that both of them are slightly true.

The first is that back in the 1930s, Bobby Jones, a golfer who had 13 majors under his belt, and banker and club chairman Clifford Roberts, who were together responsible for the creation of the golf course at Augusta and the Masters tournament, attended a dinner at the Royal Liverpool Golf Club in the UK. The captains of the club were all resplendent in matching jackets that marked out their elevated status, and that set Jones thinking …

As a result, in 1937, four years after the first Masters, Augusta members were encouraged to wear green jackets during the tournament so that the people coming to the course could give them the respect they deserved.

The other story is that Clifford Roberts wanted a way to quickly identify who members of the public could ask for directions and suchlike, and so he suggested that members all wear bright green jackets.

Either way, it wasn't until 1949, when Sam Snead was presented with an honorary green jacket for winning the Masters, that everyone thought it was a jolly good idea. And just like that, a tradition was created.

There are a couple of wrinkles in management of the jacket: winners are allowed to keep their jackets for a year before bringing them back to Augusta at the next tournament, where they are kept in perpetuity. As honorary members, former winners are entitled to wear the jacket whenever they are back at the Florida club.

This also means that anyone who wins the jacket multiple

times is actually presented with the same jacket each time they win, which is part of the reason why golfers at the top of their game tend to stay trim, because there would be nothing more embarrassing than being presented with the famous jacket only to find that it's got a little tight.

Even in a deeply structured sport like golf, there's always one, though. South Africa's Gary Player won his green jacket in 1961 but forgot to bring it home to Augusta a year later. When asked for the jacket by Clifford Roberts, Player allegedly said something along the lines of: If you want it, you'd better go and get it. At which point, Player was given a dispensation on the proviso that he never wore the jacket in public.

He did eventually take it back to Augusta, which is just as well because he won it two more times.

Dinner winners

Another way that the Master's shows off a quirky side that slightly undermines golf's traditional reputation is the tradition of the Champion's Dinner. This takes place at Augusta on the Tuesday before the championship and brings together the great and good of golf for a nosebag and a chinwag (some food and a natter).

It's hosted by (and paid for) the champion from the year before, but before you start thinking that they get the rum end of the deal, they do also get to choose the menu.

Players tend to use it to show off the cuisine of their home region, with Jon Rahm going big on the northern Spanish Basque cuisine in 2024, Scottie Scheffler wheeling out the cheeseburgers in 2013 and Hideki Matsuyama delivering platefuls of sushi in 2022.

Ben Hogan instituted the tradition in 1952, and golfers have enjoyed a range of dinners in the years in between. Looking back on the British contributions, we can all take pride in the fact that Nick Faldo served tomato soup and fish and chips in 1997 while Sandy Lyle stunned everyone in 1989 with haggis, neeps and tatties. Not to be outdone, Ian Woosnam really put the chefs through their paces with a menu that included leek and potato soup. Britain's reputation as a global culinary powerhouse is assured.

To be fair, the menus do not appear to have been all that elaborate twenty-five years ago, with Bernhard Langer offering wiener schnitzel in 1986 and the appetisingly described turkey and dressing in 1994.

If none of that appeals, guests are apparently also welcome to pick a dinner from the club's standard menu.

GARY PLAYER
(SOUTH AFRICA)

Gary Player was only the third golf player to win a career Grand Slam after Ben Hogan and Gene Sarazen, an achievement that has only been matched by three more players: Jack Nicklaus, Tiger Woods and Rory McIlroy.

He won the Open Championship's Claret Jug three times, in 1959, 1968 and 1974, the Masters' green jacket three times in 1961 (see page 122), 1974 and 1978, the PGA Championship twice in 1962 and 1972, and the US Open once, in 1965. In total, he registered 159 professional wins during a career that blossomed just as television coverage of golf was expanding.

Player has continued to play well into his 80s, and took the opening shot at the 2024 Masters, a sweet drive right down the middle of the first fairway. He puts his longevity down to an early and continued focus on fitness alongside practice on the golf course. He is also said to have an ice bath each morning.

In 1985, Player began competing in the Senior PGA Tour (now known as the Champion's Tour) and kept playing tournament golf until 2009.

He simultaneously followed the traditional career progression of poacher turned gamekeeper, launching a successful career as a golf course designer, with his company delivering more than 400 golf courses in 41 countries since the 1980s.

★ TEED OFF ★

Playing a round of golf requires several different skills, but undoubtedly one of the most demanding is the first shot. Stepping up to the tee, drawing back, connecting with the ball and following through. Everyone is equal until that shot is played. But what sets that shot apart from everything else on the fairway? It's the humble tee that elevates the ball ever so slightly so that your driver can work to its maximum potential.

Prior to the development of the modern tee, the first shot of the round would be played off a small mound of sand, which players had to take from a box at the tee area, with players wetting their hands to make the sand damp enough to mould into a pyramid shape. Alternatively, they cut a slice in the turf to raise a divot out of the ground and played off that. England's Laura Davies, who has lifted four major women's trophies, uses this technique even today.

The problem with the sand technique is that it is a messy old business, and it's hard to see greenkeepers appreciating every player on the course cutting a divot before every tee shot. As a result, in the 1890s, the rising popularity of golf and the emergence of new materials drove a period of rapid development in the science of tees.

This included the development of the combined tee/score card, a cardboard affair that could be folded into a cone to play from and then unfolded to write on the scores. It would be fascinating to know how many of this kind of tee made it to the end of a game of golf without becoming illegible.

The current tee shape didn't arrive until 1921 with the 'Reddy Tee', developed by an American dentist, William Lowell Sr, and patented in 1925. The materials used have changed in the subsequent century, but the design has stayed pretty much identical since – presumably because it's cheap to manufacture, simple to use and does exactly what it needs to do.

Unfortunately for this book, there isn't really an entertainingly quirky story attached to the development of the tee. Lowell Sr cracked the design, formed a company to sell it and might have retired rich if he hadn't been forced to spend so much of his time and resources defending his intellectual capital from similar products being marketed by competitors.

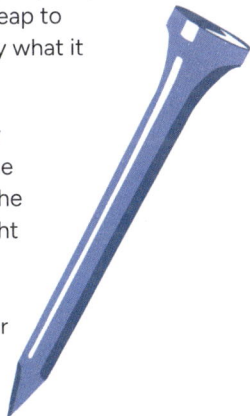

Player	Country	Wins
Miguel Ángel Jiménez (1992–2014)	Spain	21
Sam Torrance (1976–1998)	Scotland	21
José María Olazábal (1986–2005)	Spain	23
Lee Westwood (1996–2020)	England	25
Ernie Els (1994–2013)	South Africa	28
Ian Woosnam (1982–1997)	Wales	29
Nick Faldo (1977–1996)	England	30
Colin Montgomerie (1989–2007)	Scotland	31
Tiger Woods (1997–2019)	United States	41
Bernhard Langer (1980–2002)	Germany	42
Seve Ballesteros (1976–1995)	Spain	50

★ MOST MEN'S ★
EUROPEAN TOURS WON

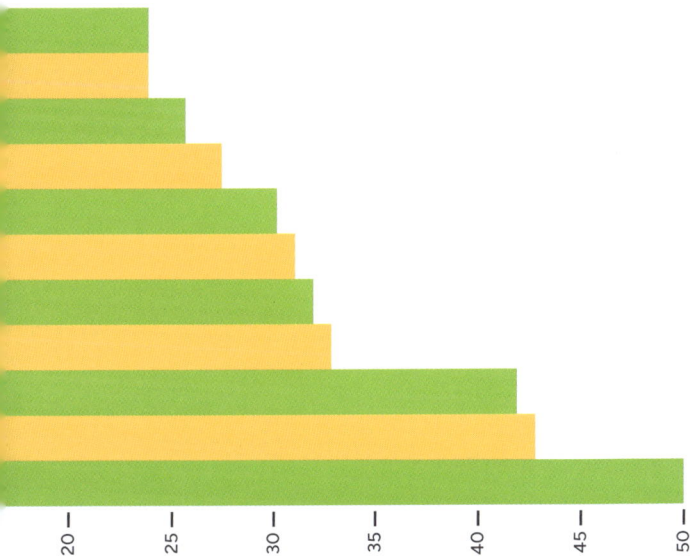

20 — 25 — 30 — 35 — 40 — 45 — 50 —

JACK NICKLAUS
(USA)

Jack Nicklaus, affectionately known as 'the Golden Bear', is widely accepted to be one of golf's GOATs (greatest-of-all-time players). Coming to prominence at the end of the 1950s and early 1960s with a pair of US Amateur titles, he won a total of 117 professional titles over the course of his career. Eighteen of those titles were in major championships – one of the rare instances in golf where his record has not been broken by Tiger Woods.

He won the US Open in 1962, 1967, 1972 and 1980, the Masters Championship in 1963, 1965, 1966, 1972, 1975 and 1986, the PGA Championship in 1963, 1971, 1973, 1975 and 1980, and the Open Championship in 1966, 1970 and 1978. Count 'em up: that's a triple career Grand Slam.

He started playing golf at the tender age of 10, encouraged by his father, who had been a scratch golfer, local tennis champion and semi-professional American footballer in his youth. Nicklaus Jr was a similarly impressive all-round athlete, with scouts from college basketball teams showing an interest. Golf was always his destiny, though, and a string of junior titles started him down the path to global recognition.

Away from the fairway, he has also played an important leadership role in the game. In the late 1970s, he used his stature to encourage the golfing authorities in Britain to widen the selection procedures for the Ryder Cup to include players from Europe to ensure that the tournament remained competitive. It might well have struggled to maintain its relevance without his intervention.

Jack Nicklaus isn't the only sports all-rounder. Winner of six PGA tour competitions as well as two in Europe and two more elsewhere, Rickie Fowler's first love was motocross. He switched to the more sedate game of golf after a serious accident. Gary Woodland, winner of the 2019 US Open, got to university on a basketball scholarship before switching to golf, and Sam Byrd competed in both the baseball's World Series and golf's Masters Tournament in the 1940s. And Ash Barty, a former world tennis number one, has also been a professional cricketer and won her local golf tournament.

★ A CHEQUERED PAST: GOLF'S ★ RELATIONSHIP WITH FASHION

Golf has a certain reputation where fashion is concerned. It might not be a totally fair reputation, but since when did fair have anything to do with reputation?

In the early days of golf, fashion was purely function. A stout coat and decent trousers tucked into your socks was the best way to avoid shivering your way around 18 holes on the links, where high winds are possible and long grass was probable. Knickerbockers and plus fours (they are technically different, don't write in) make sense in this environment because you don't really want your trouser bottoms dragging in the dew if you are going to be on the course for three and some hours.

One of the challenges for golfing clothes is that if you *are* out on the course for any length of time, there's a decent chance that you will find yourself under at least two weather fronts. This means your clothing needs to be flexible. There's a chance of rain, so you need to be as waterproof as possible. There's a hope of sun, so you need a peaked cap so that you can swing a club without blinding yourself. And if the sun does decide to put in an appearance, you need to be able to change into appropriate clothes quickly and with as little fuss as possible so you don't hold up the people trying to play behind you.

It's a long list of requirements, and marrying the functional needs with a little bit of style has been something that generations of golfers have faced.

And if you want to see some more …

Some history books suggest that by the 1920s, golf was starting to have an impact on fashion, rather than the other way around (this is the kind of history book that concerns itself with the important stuff like fashion and sport rather than the trivia of politics, monarchs and economics). The Oxford bag, the large trousers that gentlemen of the 1920s enjoyed wearing, have been suggested to be the result of golf's influence on society. The story goes that Oxford University lecturers became fed up with their undergraduates showing up to lectures in their plus fours as if they were just popping in for a quick bit of academia between rounds of golf. The mardy dons got plus fours banned from the quads.

Undeterred, the golf-mad students of the age simply had their trousers expanded so that they could wear their golfing attire underneath. With a quick Bucks Fizz-at-Eurovision-style flourish, they could reveal their plus fours and were ready to make a dash for the first hole as soon as the bell went (or whatever happens at those stratospheric heights of education). These voluminous trousers became known as 'Oxford bags', and pretty soon everyone from Members of Parliament in the UK right the way through to gangsters in Chicago in the US were joyfully doing the lindy hop in golf-influenced trousers.

Sadly, the story may not be entirely true because fashion historians have suggested that the earliest forms of Oxford bags would not have been big enough to squeeze in a cheeky pair of plus fours. According to the experts, it's possible that Oxford bags grew out of the university's rowing club because they could slip over a pair of rowing shorts. Either way, while golf may get the blame in some quarters for history's most ludicrously oversized trousers, it's probably not actually the culprit.

Make everything louder than everything else

The reality is that while golf is sometimes perceived as having a fashion problem, the legendary clashes of houndstooth and plaid were only really witnessed during the late 1970s and early 1980s – and simply reflected the somewhat garish fashions of the time.

Blame television. Colour TV came along at the same time as a generation of superb golfers arose and as new production techniques were making it possible to make garments more vibrant than they had been in the past. Golf became fashionable just as everything became more colourful.

Admittedly, there was also a generation of male middle managers taking refuge on the golf courses up and down the land whose idea of fashion didn't go much further than knowing how to pair a shirt with a tie, and whose partners were simply glad that they were getting some fresh air at the weekend and didn't really care what they were wearing because they didn't have to stand anywhere near them ... but that's perhaps something for the social history books.

Either way, things were loud in the 1980s on the golf course because things were loud in the 1980s. In the main, things have calmed down a lot since then; and in the main, that's probably not a bad thing.

Glorious beige

From a fashion point of view, it feels like golf is enjoying a golden age. It's an age where people can focus on the game — the majesty of the drives and the feats on the green — without being given a headache by accidentally looking at the clothes the people they are playing a round with are wearing.

Away from the golf course, athleisure — the portmanteau word that combines 'athletics' with 'leisure' and was probably invented by a very expensive consultant — continues to be a significant presence on the high street. This means the clothes that a lot of people wear when they are out and about are often suitable for the golf course (although some clubs have very strict dress codes, and it's always worth checking before you turn up head to toe in Hoodrich clobber).

It's also worth noting that the rise of sponsorship has also removed a lot of the fashion peril from golf. These days brands have a lot of say about how their logos are worn and where they are seen, and to an extent players have to go along with it if they want to enjoy the benefits of sponsorship.

In some ways, golf's current blend of understated style and focus on utility might lack some of the boisterousness of the 1980s (where you could walk into a room and instantly spot the golfer), but that's the price of progress!

Checkered history?

Pringle and its argyle pattern were almost synonymous with golf in the 1980s, but the relationship stretches back a lot further than that. The company was set up in 1815 in Harwick on the Scottish borders where they focused on making stockings and, sensibly, long johns, before making the move to cardigans and the like shortly after World War I.

It also appears that women started pinching their husbands' cardigans at almost the same time because they were, frankly, very practical. The experts at Pringle are also said to have used their expertise in practical undergarments to pave the way for one of the other important changes in women's fashion in the early 1920s, as restrictive corsets were pinged away in favour of lighter, more liberated garb. Mostly so they could play golf more comfortably.

The argyle pattern started popping up in the 1920s but really took off in the 1960s, peaked in the 1980s before fading into irony subsequently.

"A leading difficulty with the average player is that he totally misunderstands what is meant by concentration. He may think he is concentrating hard when he is merely worrying."

Lawyer and noted amateur golfer Bobby Jones, who helped set up both the Augusta National Golf Club and the Masters Tournament, knew about pressure and how to deal with it.

★ CHOKED BY THE YIPS ★

Golf can be a lonely sport: An isolated battle against your opponent, the course designer, the elements, and most of all, yourself. We've all had it; you approach a shot you've made a hundred times, you move up to address the ball, and that little voice in your head - the one with a tone that's usually so soothing - simply and quietly says "...but what if?"

The yips can strike at any time, but it's usually at the worst possible moment. You can be at the very top of your game, be given the simplest shot to make - and that voice, that simple question, opens up a tiny crack of doubt in your abilities. And once they set in they can spiral. That first, simple, shot goes awry and it all comes crashing down like a great big game of psychological jenga. You are left watching the person that you should have easily beaten walking off with the prize that should have been yours.

Sports psychologists have several long, intelligent and Latin-derived names for it, but we all know it by its true name - the yips.

Interestingly they may not be completely in your head, it's possible that they are caused, or at least made worse, by a physical condition that affects muscles that have been honed to do one specific thing. The next time you try to do that thing, the muscles give a tiny twitch and that twitch just knocks you off enough to muck up that shot. So you tense up, and as a result you can't make the next shot, or the one after that...

The yips are too complicated and their causes too varied to even try and off a full explanation in this book, but if you do find yourself suffering from them, remember that it's estimated between a quarter and a half of golfers will experience the phenomenon at some point. Bernhard Langer suffered from them so badly when he was 18 he is said to have thought about quitting the game. Ben Hogan started freezing over the ball as he was trying to make a putt, and the more he found himself doing it, the more he knew that people were noticing and the more embarrassed he became. The list goes on ... So if you get them, just try and remember that you are in esteemed company.

★ CADDIE OR CADDY? ★

Golf is a sport that evolved in Britain, was embraced by the US and then conquered the world. It has two major authorities: one based in Britain, the other based in the US. In this sort of situation, there is usually a very quiet, very polite tussle over the dictionary: 'motorway' or 'freeway'; 'gas' or 'petrol'; 'organisation' or 'organization'; 'colour' or 'color'; 'football' or 'soccer'. In the commentary of the 1979 Open Championship, when Seve Ballesteros thumped his drive into what the American commentator called a 'parking lot', his English colleague quickly, and politely, corrected him to 'car park'.

Anyway, take the word 'caddie': it's crying out for two different spellings. In any consistent world, one side of the Atlantic would spell it one way, and the other would pointedly spell it the other way.

Golf, though, appears to take pleasure in confounding expectations, and there appears to be little argument over the caddie/caddy debate. Both the USGA in America and the Royal & Ancient in Britain are agreed: the person who carries the clubs is a caddie.

If only everything in life was so simple.

As for where the word comes from, it's thought to be a Scottishisation(/Scottishization) of the French word 'cadet'. There are some who suggest it was the august Mary, Queen of Scots – noted golfer, queen in the north and a casket of trouble in the south – who coined the phrase. Her clubs were said to have been carried by military cadets; from there, the word 'cadets' is said to have been simplified to 'caddie'. To be fair, royalty has a tendency to claim credit for anything it comes into contact with, but either way, she played golf and the word entered the lexicon during her reign.

★ GREG NORMAN ★
(AUSTRALIA)

Greg Norman arose from Australia in the mid-1970s, earning a reputation for assertive golf that was a pleasure to watch. Without putting too fine a point on it, he could really wallop a golf ball, driving off the tee in a way that had his opponents looking around nervously.

He won the Open Championship twice (in 1986 and 1993), and was snapping right at the heels of the eventual victors at eight other majors. He won a total of 20 PGA Tour events, 14 on the European Tour, two in Japan, 33 on the PGA Tour of Australasia, and 21 sundry others, and finished in the top 10 in 30 of the majors that he entered. Basically, it's a pretty impressive *résumé* of professional golfing achievements.

The challenge is that it was very nearly so much more. To come second in any of the world's four major golf events is massively impressive. To come second eight times without getting over the line seems cruel. It had to happen to someone, and Norman seems to have a thick enough hide to deal with it.

★ STANDING ★ IN THE WAY OF CHANGE

Golf has a delicate balance that needs to be maintained, particularly in these days of fast-evolving technology. The sport needs to protect the par and handicap systems so that it remains just difficult enough to present a challenge and so scores can be compared back at the clubhouse without too many eyebrows being raised.

At the same time, it has to be adaptable to change and evolution, not least because the people who have tried to obstruct some changes have run the risk of being swept away.

Allan Robertson (see page 34) had an apparently unbeatable golfing partnership with his apprentice Old Tom Morris (although at this point Morris wasn't actually old), but the relationship was put under massive strain when Morris was caught playing with a guttie ball rather than one of Robertson's feathery-leatheries (see page 16). Robertson thought, rightly, that the guttie balls were a threat to his centuries-old family business, but he tried to stand in the way of change rather than go with it. In the end, the future had its way and Robertson's company had to stop producing feathery-leatheries and move to gutties.

Fifty years later, the British golfing establishment tried to stop the Haskell ball from making its way over the pond. The "Bounding Billy" ball was seen by some in Britain as an innovation too far, that it would make golf too easy and force the redesign of courses. It wasn't an outright ban, but the Haskell was prohibited from being used at professional tournaments.

Unfortunately, Haskell balls were cheap, consistent and improved quickly, so people flocked to use them so that they could improve their game; in the end, the British golfing establishment had to suck it up.

Golf teaches many lessons. Knowing when to accept change is hopefully one of them.

That said...

Of course, golf naturally goes out of its way to confound the valuable life lessons, even when they are lessons the sport taught in the first place.

At the end of 2023, the Royal & Ancient and the United States Golf Association announced that they were going to change the rules surrounding golf balls to try and reduce the relentless enhancements in aerodynamics and all-round performance that have been witnessed over the last half a century.

The initial discussions suggested that only elite players would be covered by the new rules, but it's been extended to avoid confusion and to ensure a level playing field. The concern was that the game's authorities could have created a situation where two rules were having to be enforced, which would have been confusing and difficult to police. As a result, the new rules, which will come into force in 2028 for professionals and 2030 for the rest of us mortals, will apply to all players.

A mere 5%

Hopefully you've reached the point in this book where you don't expect a very detailed, technical analysis of the changes, but what we can tell you is that in the future balls won't travel as far — in theory by about 5% or around 10-15 metres.

The reason for the rule change is similar to the attempt back in the early 20th century when the Haskell arrived (see page 21); using modern balls, top-level players can hit the ball further than the majority of course designers envisaged, so there's a risk that the fairway are becoming too easy for too many players.

If the balls are making it easier to hit the ball further, then the logical thing to do is to extend the fairways. The challenge there, though, is that in many parts of the world, particularly in urban and semi-urban areas, there is pressure on land use which is pushing prices up.

Added to this are the environmental and economic considerations. Maintaining a golf course requires attention and a lot of water, and both attention and water cost money. So while the simple option would be to make fairways 5% longer to keep up with technology and the mighty hitters, it's all a little more complicated.

How this change will play out will be fascinating.

Come back for the 2125 edition and we'll let you know.

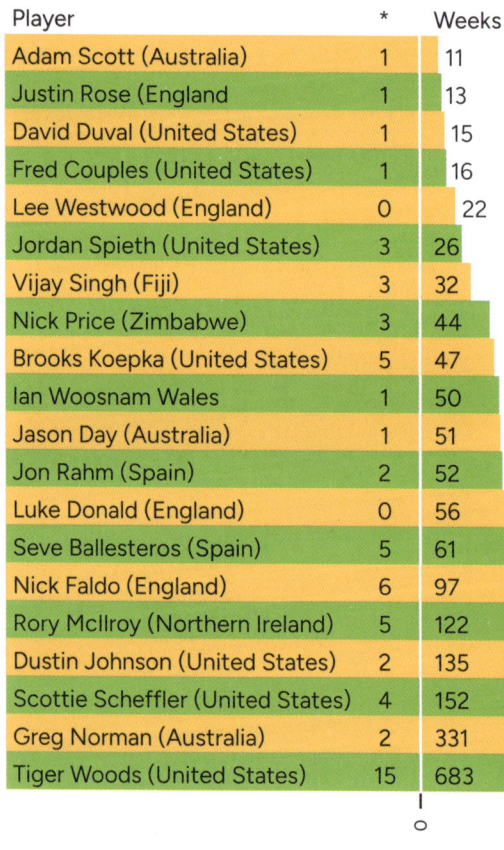

Player	*	Weeks
Adam Scott (Australia)	1	11
Justin Rose (England	1	13
David Duval (United States)	1	15
Fred Couples (United States)	1	16
Lee Westwood (England)	0	22
Jordan Spieth (United States)	3	26
Vijay Singh (Fiji)	3	32
Nick Price (Zimbabwe)	3	44
Brooks Koepka (United States)	5	47
Ian Woosnam Wales	1	50
Jason Day (Australia)	1	51
Jon Rahm (Spain)	2	52
Luke Donald (England)	0	56
Seve Ballesteros (Spain)	5	61
Nick Faldo (England)	6	97
Rory McIlroy (Northern Ireland)	5	122
Dustin Johnson (United States)	2	135
Scottie Scheffler (United States)	4	152
Greg Norman (Australia)	2	331
Tiger Woods (United States)	15	683

0   100

★ WEEKS AS GOLF'S ★ NUMBER ONE MALE PLAYER

*number of majors

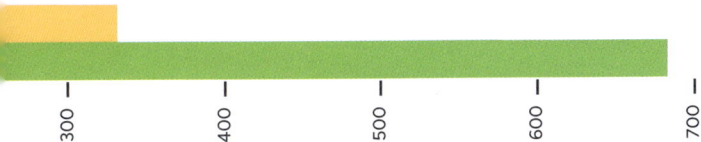

300	400	500	600	700

★ IT'S GOLF, BUT CRAYZEE ★

Crazy golf is not golf. Golf is a considered game, full of subtlety, that pits the player in a battle of wits against the course designer, the elements, and themselves. It's a blend of club control, alignment of the body, skill, practice and luck.

Crazy golf is something that people do when they really want to have a massive family argument but don't have the imagination to start one. It's a powder keg of testosterone, bitter resentments and abject boredom that brings out the stereotypes in all of us. The overly competitive one starts it, the petulant one follows, the one who has been driven beyond exasperation steps in and make an angry plea for sanity, and nobody notices the sad, quiet one, who just wishes that everyone would stop shouting. They all emerge as soon as you step over the threshold into the land of dubious delights that is the crazy golf course.

It is sometimes said that golf is responsible for more family strife than any other activity because players can become obsessive about their game. It's simply not true. Even a bad round of golf helps people take a moment to step away from their troubles and live in the moment. They return home refreshed and happy. Crazy golf, on the other hand, was invented by evil doers.

★ THE INTRODUCTION OF ★ THE HANDICAP SYSTEM

It was the Ladies Golf Union (LGU) in 1893 that gave the first serious push towards a recognised handicap allocation based on an agreed par system across Britain. One of the things that started to give the handicap system traction was that the LGU sent people out across women's courses to encourage enforcement. This helped players embrace the system and understand the value of being able to compare scores between competitors.

There was naturally a lot of derision from golf's fraternity, based not least on the fact that the system seems to have been a pretty good first effort and the chaps were a bit put out that they hadn't thought of it first. It was the 1890s and, so far as the brotherhood was concerned, women weren't technically supposed to be having good ideas for at least another century.

Two years later, the men's game in England made its first attempt at creating and enforcing a system based on what the LGU had developed. The English approach gradually spread to Scotland and then the world.

★ TIGER WOODS ★
(USA)

Tiger Woods has been an extraordinary golfer throughout his career. If you look at most of the records set by golfers prior to his rise, most have been broken by Woods during his frankly phenomenal dominance of the game between the late 1990s and the mid-noughties. 82 PGA Tour titles. 15 majors. Awesome.

Woods has had his name engraved on 110 professional trophies, including the Masters five times (1997, 2001, 2002, 2005 and 2019), the PGA Championship four times (1999, 2000, 2006 and 2007), the US Open three times (2000, 2002 and 2008) and the Open Championship three times (2000, 2005 and 2006). In short, this means that he's technically enjoyed three career Grand Slams of Golf's four major tournaments. So far.

Woods' talent was clear from an early age. He made his first television appearance in 1978 at the grand old age of two (yup) on *The Mike Douglas Show* alongside comedian Bob Hope and actor Jimmy Stewart, making a decent drive off a tee in the studio.

Six years later, Woods recorded his first hole in one. Gloriously, the eight-year-old was too small to see the hole from the tee and had to be picked up so he could get the angle to see that there really was no ball visible on the green. Having realised his achievement, he ran to the hole, picked out his ball in triumph and was promptly told that he'd forgotten his golf bag and needed to go back and get it from the tee.

More importantly, he won the US Junior Championship three times in a row and the US Amateur Championship three times in a row between 1994 and 1996.

Injury has blighted his last few years, but he still draws a crowd whenever he plays, and his name is likely to stay on many pages of golf's record book for years to come.

Tiger Woods is not the only golfing child prodigy. Michelle Wie began playing in Hawaii at the age of four, became the youngest player to qualify for an LPGA event at 12, turned pro at 15 and won five LPGA Tour events before her career was curtailed by injury. Jordan Spieth meanwhile was number one in the AJGA Golf Rankings before turning 19 and is the second youngest golfer to win the masters.

★ THE FUTURE OF GOLF ★

At the moment, the sport of golf is at something of a crossroads, with alternatives for its future being put forward. Some might even go so far as to say competing visions of its future.

At the time of writing, the alternatives are still being talked about. While some of the initial bad feeling appears to have cooled, there is a long way to go before there is likely to be anything approaching certainty around what the future may hold.

There's a moment between past and future where it's all about the interrelationships and the politics. At this moment, it's impossible to say how it will play out, but the one thing that there is little doubt about is that the game of golf will survive. It brings too much pleasure to the millions around the world who follow it and play it for it not to.

★ THE UNSUNG HERO THAT ★ MADE GOLF POSSIBLE

There are many factors that led to the 19th century's sporting boom in the UK. Primarily, everyone was looking at the success of cricket and thinking, how could we be doing that with our sport. Then there was the fact that the roads were improving, making it easier for things to happen between villages and towns as the years went on. Improved communication was also part of this, helping sets of rules become nationalised rather than be confined to local or regional areas.

In the case of golf though, the single most important factor was probably the creation of the humble mechanical lawnmower.

In the dark days of the before times, grass was long and difficult to play. There were sheep that could chew the grass down, but they had too much of a mind of their own to go where green keepers wanted them to go, and not enough minds of their own to listen when someone shouted 'fore' at them. There were also teams of people mooching about the fairways with scythes or crawling down the greens with scissors, snipping individual blades of grass every day during the growing season. Neither sheep nor people were cheap, even in them there days.

Hooray for Budding

In 1830 though, Edwin Beard Budding of Stroud in the Cotswolds invented the mechanical lawnmower. Various versions were created, the some of which had to be horse drawn because they were really heavy.

It took sixty years of refinement to get to a lawnmower that could be operated under its own steam (literally, it was steam powered), and did away with the need for horses. The world was still a long way from modern convenience though, with the engines taking up to 10 minutes to heat up so that they could start moving.

They were also very expensive, technical machines, so groundsmen had to be good keeping them in working order if they were going to keep the greens up to scratch.

Golf courses used to sing with the sound of labourers trying to get the grass a proper height, then they were alive with the sound of horses dragging mechanical mowers. They were drowned out by chunter of steam engines, which in turn was replaced by the sound of small petrol engines. Currently we have the quiet hum of robots and their electric motors, but who knows what comes next.

"Show me a man with a great golf game, and I'll show you a man who has been neglecting something."

John F. Kennedy.